Antichrist and Judgment Day

Antichrist and Judgment Day

The Middle French
Jour du Jugement

Translated with Introduction and Commentary
by Richard K. Emmerson and David F. Hult

With a Note on the Music by Keith Glaeske

Early European Drama Translation Series

Martin Stevens, Founding Editor
Stephen K. Wright, General Editor

Pegasus Press
University of North Carolina at Asheville
Asheville, North Carolina
1998

©Copyright 1998
Pegasus Press
Asheville, North Carolina

Library of Congress Cataloging-in-Publications Data

Jour du jugement. English.
   Antichrist and Judgment day : the Middle French Jour du Jugement
translated with introduction and commentary by Richard K. Emmerson
and David F. Hult : with a note on the music by Keith Glaeske.
   p.   cm. --(Early European drama translation series)
Includes bibliographical references.
   ISBN 1-889818-06-2 (pbk.)
   1. Judgment Day--Drama.   2. Mysteries and miracle-plays. French-
-Translations into English.   3. Mysteries and miracle-plays, French-
-History and criticism.   4. Judgment Day in literature.
   I. Emmerson, Richard Kenneth. II. Hult, David F., 1952- .
III. Glaeske, Keith. IV. Title. V. Series.
   PQ1349.J6813   1998
   842'.1--dc21   98-33663
                              CIP

This book is made to last.
It is printed on acid-free paper
to library specifications.
The typeface is Palatino.

Printed in the United States of America

The Early European Drama Translation Series

The Early European Drama Translation Series is a project established under the auspices of the Medieval and Renaissance Drama Society. The purpose of the EEDT series is to provide reliable, inexpensive translations of major European vernacular plays from the Middle Ages and Renaissance for use in a wide variety of undergraduate and graduate courses. It is the explicit intent of the series to internationalize the teaching and study of the early theater by supplying translations of important texts from many genres: mystery plays, saint plays, history plays, miracles, moralities, folk plays, carnival plays, processionals, and civic and ecclesiastical ceremonies of every kind.

Martin Stevens and Stephen K. Wright are Founding Editor and General Editor of the EEDT series, respectively. Members of the Advisory Board include Kathleen Ashley, Konrad Eisenbichler, Kathleen Falvey, Gordon Kipling, Alan E. Knight, Robert Potter, and Eckehard Simon.

Volume One: *Arnoul Gréban, The Mystery of the Passion: The Third Day,* translated by Paula Giuliano

Volume Two: *Antichrist and Judgment Day: The Middle French "Jour du Jugement,"* translated by Richard K. Emmerson and David F. Hult

Volume Three: *Medieval Dutch Drama: Four Secular Plays and Four Farces from the Van Hulthem Manuscript,* translated by Johanna C. Prins

Contents

Preface   viii

Introduction

    The Play   ix

    Structure   xi

    Manuscript, Date, and Provenance   xiii

    Theological Contexts   xvi

    Antichrist and Doomsday in Medieval Drama   xix

    Staging   xxii

    The Miniatures   xxxiii

    A Note on the Translation   xxxiv

    Facsimile Pages   xxxiv

Translation: *The Day of Judgment*   1

Appendices

    1: Sample Text from Besançon 579   89

    2: List of Miniatures in Besançon 579   94

    3: The Music in Besançon 579,   99
       by Keith Glaeske

Bibliography   105

Preface

This volume has a long history. It originates in our friendship, dating back to the early seventies, when we were graduate students at Stanford University and enrolled in a course studying Old French. Although our separate careers took us in different directions, by meeting at professional conferences we managed to keep our friendship alive and to continue to share our mutual interests in medieval literature. Once in the early nineties, over breakfast at the International Medieval Congress at Western Michigan University, we discussed the possibility of translating the *Jour du Jugement* for the newly established Early European Drama Translation Series, and the project took off from there. We are delighted to present this fascinating play in translation; we hope that it will be welcomed not only by students and teachers, but also scholars and directors.

We wish to express our gratitude to several individuals who have been supportive of this project. We thank the librarians of the Bibliothèque Municipale, Besançon, for access to MS 579 and for permission to publish its facsimile pages; Stephen K. Wright, for his steady support and useful advice; and Pamela Sheingorn, for testing portions of the translation with her students in a graduate seminar on medieval drama and for making helpful comments at an early stage. We are grateful to Robert L. A. Clark and Graham A. Runnalls, who provided careful and detailed readings of the introduction, translation, and commentary, making many useful suggestions that have improved the volume. We also appreciate the expert assistance of Keith Glaeske with the music of the manuscript; we are pleased to publish his discussion of the music as appendix 3.

Richard Emmerson wishes to acknowledge the support provided by Western Washington University in the form of a summer research grant in 1995 and a Bureau of Faculty Research grant used to purchase photographs of the manuscript's miniatures. David Hult wishes to acknowledge the University of Virginia's support of this project in the form of a summer research grant in 1993 and a Sesquicentennial Faculty Fellowship in Fall 1994, which provided release time from teaching and administrative duties at a crucial stage in the translation.

Introduction

THE PLAY

The Middle French play, the *Jour du Jugement*, is the only medieval play that stages at length and in detail two of the most fundamental episodes of Christian eschatology, the appearance of Antichrist in the last days and the Last Judgment. The play's title is not medieval, but was coined by its modern editor, Émile Roy, based on a reference in the play, "Ce est dou jour dou jugement" (l. 8).[1] Given the full range of the play's action, perhaps a more accurate title would be *Antichrist and Judgment Day*, but, to avoid confusion, we will continue to refer to the play by its traditional title.

The *Jour du Jugement* is spectacular in its breadth and its theatricality, representing scenes in Hell and Heaven as well as on Earth, in Babylon and the Earthly Paradise as well as in Europe. Extant in 2,438 octosyllabic lines rhyming in couplets, it originally was somewhat longer, at least 2,700 to 2,800 lines. Its cast of ninety-three characters is enormous, including ten devils, ten angels, and ten kings; the pope, two cardinals, and a bishop; a host of Jews, soldiers, and other followers of Antichrist; numerous saints of the New Testament and two Old Testament figures, Enoch and Elijah; the righteous saved and many more of the evil damned, who, at Doomsday, repent of their sins too late; and Antichrist and his mother, the "whore of Babylon," as well as Christ and his mother, the Virgin Mary. Although focusing on the eschatological conclusion of history on earth, the play covers the entire span of salvation history, beginning with the Preacher's introductory sermon, which recounts the Fall of Adam and Eve, and concluding with the fiery destruction of the world, the consignment of the damned to Hell, and the reward of the righteous in Heaven. Yet it also reflects contemporary social interests, as evident in its treatment of the Usurer, various ecclesiastics, and the Jews.

The play is filled with several contrasts: between the depersonalized angels, who are simply numbered rather than given names, and the devils, with their symbolic names; between those who are deceived by Antichrist and thereby temporarily gain by their support of the hypocritical tyrant, and

---

[1] *Le Jour du Jugement*, ed. Roy, 21.

those who remain faithful to Christ and die for their beliefs; between the hellish origins of Antichrist in a demonic conspiracy to gain control of the Church, and the punishment of the wicked and reward of the righteous resulting from the heavenly power of Christ; between Antichrist's mother, who plays the role of the apocalyptic "Whore of Babylon" (Apoc. 17), and Christ's mother, Mary, who as Queen of Heaven and Mother of God intercedes with her son at Doomsday. In developing such binary oppositions, the play is typical of Christian theological discourse in general and of the dualism inherent in apocalypticism in particular, which understands history as an elaboration of the cosmic conflict between good and evil, ultimately to be settled at the end of time with Christ's separation of the saved and the damned during the Last Judgment.

Although based on theological teachings and popular expectations regarding the last things that were long established in Christian belief, the play also reflects attitudes more typical of the later Middle Ages. For example, in its treatment of the Jews, the play takes for granted and develops the anti-Semitism that was rampant in medieval Europe in general and that is a feature of apocalypticism specifically.[2] The Apocalypse uses the term, "Synagogue of Satan" (Apoc. 2:9, 3:9), to identify the opponents of Christ, so that anti-Semitism became part and parcel of medieval eschatology, and the Jews became key players in the events of the last days. Although in some accounts the Jews are expected to be converted to Christianity, the *Jour du Jugement* consistently represents them as evil, as the first and most faithful supporters of Antichrist. The play also includes elements of the anticlericalism evident in much late medieval vernacular literature. Of its clerical characters, for example, only the Pope remains faithful when confronted by Antichrist, and one ecclesiastic, the Evil Bishop, is an early and very active supporter of Antichrist. Among the resurrected, moreover, are a lecherous Bishop, Abbess, and Prioress, whose sins reflect popular rumors about the hypocrisy of the religious. Finally, the *Jour du Jugement* seems to oppose the growing profit economy of the later Middle Ages. It treats Antichrist's control of the world in economic terms, for example, shown through his minting and monopoly of coins, and it is particularly hostile to the practice of usury, damning to Hell not only a Usurer but his entire household. Even Antichrist shows some distaste for usury, when Annes, speaking on the deceiver's behalf, declares that no one should give the new coinage more value than Antichrist has specified (ll. 658–61).

Despite these contemporary social and economic interests, however, the play is not political in the narrow sense; it does not allude to specific ecclesiastical or partisan arguments or crises. It is not, for example, as Roy

[2] See, for example, Langmuir, *Toward a Definition of Antisemitism*.

unsuccessfully sought to show, an allegory mirroring the complex events surrounding the Great Schism within the Church of the late fourteenth century.[3] It is less concerned with the local and contemporary political scene than it is with the worldwide challenge of evil that Christians expected in the imminent future. Although its concerns are timely, the *Jour du Jugement* is primarily interested in the timeless issues of Christian eschatology.

STRUCTURE

Since the plot is complex, an outline of its major "scenes" may be helpful. It is important, though, to keep in mind that the manuscript does not specify any scenic divisions and that the action flows smoothly and without interruption from beginning to end. In order not to impede that flow, we have not provided scene headings or numbers in the translation. The following outline, which identifies those points, is provided only for summary and analytical purposes:

Prologue

1. Preacher's sermon (ll. 1–192)

Birth of Antichrist

2. Parliament in Hell (ll. 193–265)
3. Engignart and Agrappart travel to Babylon (ll. 266–87)
4. Seduction of Antichrist's Mother (ll. 288–341)
5. Celebration in Hell (ll. 342–65)
6. Birth of Antichrist (ll. 366–421)
7. Second celebration in Hell (ll. 422–45)
8. Antichrist as a baby (ll. 446–55)

Career of Antichrist

9. The Angel summons Enoch and Elijah from the Earthly Paradise (ll. 456–77)
10. Enoch and Elijah preach against Antichrist (ll. 478–537)

---

[3] *Jour du Jugement*, ed. Roy, 119–56. Beginning with the review of Roy's edition by Valois in *Journal des Savants*, Roy's political interpretation of the play has been largely discarded, and in his *Le Mystère de la passion en France du xiv* au xvi* siècle* (Dijon: Université de Dijon, 1903), Roy withdrew his original political interpretation (67*). The few scholars who have written on the play now favor readings that emphasize its development of traditional eschatology. See Aichele, 35–36; and Emmerson, *Antichrist in the Middle Ages*, 172–80.

11. Satan teaches Antichrist (ll. 538–85)
12. Antichrist's sermon (ll. 586–605)
13. Antichrist heals Blind Man (ll. 606–29)
14. Antichrist mints coins engraved with his image (ll. 630–95)
15. Antichrist heals Leper (ll. 696–743)
16. Antichrist raises dead man (ll. 744–827)
17. Ten Kings question Antichrist (ll. 828–941)
18. Antichrist distributes wealth to Four Poor Men (ll. 942–1009)
19. Ten Kings are converted (ll. 1010–41)
20. Enoch and Elijah are arrested (ll. 1042–91)
21. Enoch and Elijah are condemned and killed (ll. 1092–1201)
22. Pope and Cardinals are arrested (ll. 1202–95)
23. Pope and Cardinals before Antichrist (ll. 1296–1409)
24. Enoch and Elijah are resurrected and taken to Heaven (ll. 1410–23)
25. Responses to resurrection of Enoch and Elijah (ll. 1424–71)

Signs of the End

26. John distributes vials of wrath to Angels (ll. 1472–1511)
27. Angels pour out vials of wrath (ll. 1512–1621)
28. Responses to vials of wrath (ll. 1622–92)
29. God's plans for judgment (ll. 1693–1715)
30. Cherubim and Seraphim appeal to Mary for intercession (ll. 1716–37)
31. Saints appeal to Mary for intercession (ll. 1738–1829)
32. Mary's intercession with her Son (ll. 1830–63)
33. Four Evangelists resurrect the Dead (ll. 1864–1937)
34. Sorrow of the reprobate (ll. 1938–2029)

Last Judgment

35. Judgment on Usurer and his family (ll. 2030–75)
36. Devils take damned to Hell (ll. 2076–95)
37. Sorrow of Bishop and Prioress (ll. 2096–2156)
38. Mark and Luke gather resurrected to judgment (ll. 2157–70)
39. Christ displays signs of his passion (ll. 2171–2220)
40. Disciples sit in judgment (ll. 2221–2310)
41. Christ renders judgment (ll. 2311–79)
42. Devils take damned to Hell (ll. 2380–2411)
43. John, Luke, and Paul lead saved to Heaven (ll. 2412–38)

One way to approach the structure of the *Jour du Jugement* is to compare it with the popular Passion plays. In a sense it is linked to the themes of the Passion and serves as a sequel that ups the ante. For example, the *Passion du Palatinus*, a play of roughly the same length that represents an early stage of the Passion play, sets forth a paradigm in which evil at first appears to be victorious but is ultimately defeated by Christ. The *Palatinus* begins with the betrayal of Jesus by the Jews and his death on the Cross, which is followed by the joy and exultation of the devils; but then Christ defeats Satan during the Harrowing of Hell and is resurrected, so that the play ends with the victory of the righteous. Similarly, the *Jour du Jugement* begins with the hellish conspiracy leading to the birth of Antichrist, the Jewish support of Christ's final enemy, and the death of Enoch and Elijah, Christ's final representatives on earth. But with their resurrection the tide turns: Antichrist is defeated, Christ appears in glory, and the dead are resurrected to be judged. At its conclusion the devils, now complaining rather than dancing, are subordinate to Christ and serve his commands.

In the midst of its summary of salvation history the opening sermon of the *Jour du Jugement* links the Last Judgment to the Passion. After describing how the Crucifixion and Harrowing of Hell "opened to all virtuous people the portal / of Paradise" (ll. 68–69), it shifts suddenly from the triumphant past to the present: "But the world has declined / since that time" (ll. 71–72). In the original this shift is emphasized by the adversative *Mais* that introduces line 71. It suggests that even though the story of the Passion ends with Christ's triumph and human redemption, this is not quite enough, for evil is still rampant. The story must therefore continue. If we understand both Passion and eschatological plays as exemplary spectacles meant to persuade their audiences, they have the same goal in teaching the crucial role of Christ in salvation and in opposition to the powers of evil, but they differ strikingly in their methods. Whereas Passion plays inspire the spectators through a positive message—that Christ has opened the path to Heaven—the *Jour du Jugement* and other eschatological plays necessarily accentuate the negative, setting forth a warning to all in the last days concerning Antichrist's impending deceit and inspiring fear of fiery punishment. Thus, in this play the sinners—Antichrist, the multitude of his followers, and the vast majority of those judged—seem more important than the virtuous. Even the devils are not so much defeated but contained, remaining as eternal punishers of the damned, who by far outnumber the saved.

MANUSCRIPT, DATE, AND PROVENANCE

The *Jour du Jugement* is extant in one manuscript, Besançon, Bibliothèque Municipale, MS 579, which contains seventy-six parchment folios of about 252 x 180 mm, numbered ii + 74.[4] Folio 1^r–1^v includes a list of ninety-four

---

[4] See Castan, ed., *Catalogue général des manuscrits des bibliothèques publiques des*

characters, and fol. 2ᵛ is taken up by a full-page miniature representing the Last Judgment. The text of the play follows, written with pale black ink in a Gothic cursive in double columns on fols. 3ʳ–36ᵛ.[5] Each folio side is ruled and can accommodate fifty-six lines of text. The text is often ornamented, with burnished gold initials, blue and purplish scrolls, and rubrics in red. Particularly fascinating are the eighty-eight miniatures generally representing dramatic scenes that are painted within the columns of text. At least four folio leaves are missing, one after both fols. 26ᵛ and 28ᵛ and one or possibly more after both fols. 32ᵛ and 35ᵛ.[6] Following three blank folios (37ʳ–39ᵛ) is a second text, beginning "Ci commence le testament maistre Iehan de Meun" (fol. 40ʳ). This is the *Testament* that is usually attributed to Jean de Meun and that is frequently found collected with the *Romance of the Rose* in fourteenth- and fifteenth-century manuscripts. Probably written by a different scribe, it takes up the manuscript's remaining folios (40ʳ–74ʳ).

The dating and provenance of the manuscript is uncertain. Roy, detecting what he considered to be contemporary political allusions to the papal schism of the late fourteenth century, dated the play exactly, to Holy Friday, 5 April 1398, and the manuscript shortly thereafter.[7] But this dating, based largely on a now-rejected political interpretation of the play, is not persuasive. In fact, several of the text's linguistic features would suggest a dating in the first half of the fourteenth century, inasmuch as they reflect an especially conservative tendency with regard to the development from Old

France-Départements 32, *Besançon*, 338–39.

[5] All Latin texts that are set apart or that form an entire verse are written in Gothic letters and in red ink. These lines are not numbered in our translation.

[6] Although Roy thought that only four leaves were missing, one each after fols. 26v, 28v, 32v, and 35v, it is possible that the lacunae are much greater. Catchwords are written at the bottom of fols. 10v, 18v, 26v, and 32v, suggesting that, after the introductory materials (fols. 1ʳ–2ᵛ), the text of the original was arranged in gatherings of eight folios. The first three gatherings (fols. 3ʳ–10ᵛ, 11ʳ–18ᵛ, 19ʳ–26ᵛ) are complete; the fourth gathering (fols. 27ʳ–32ᵛ) includes only six folios, suggesting that two folios are missing, one each after fol. 26ᵛ and 28ᵛ. The fifth gathering (fols. 33ʳ–39ᵛ) now contains only seven folios. It may have originally included nine folios (i.e., a regular gathering with an added folio), from which two folios are now missing (one each after fol. 32ᵛ and 35ᵛ). But since the last three folios (fols. 37ʳ–39ᵛ) of the present fifth gathering are blank, it seems unlikely that a ninth and blank folio would have been added. The other possibility is that the present fifth gathering conflates two original gatherings of eight folios each, from which nine folios are missing, distributed after fols. 32ᵛ and 35ᵛ. This is possible from a literary point of view, because these lacunae fall at points in the text that could be (and often were in Doomsday plays) greatly expanded. The loss of nine rather than two folios from the present fifth gathering would mean that originally the Last Judgment section of the play was much longer and provided a more equal balance to the first section on Antichrist.

[7] *Jour du Jugement*, ed. Roy, 154. Roy also felt that linguistically the play could be dated to the very end of the fourteenth century, based upon what he calls the "confusion des règles" characteristic of that period (157).

to Middle French (traditionally, although somewhat arbitrarily, located around 1300). Perhaps the most important of these traits is the author's (and the scribe's) careful maintenance of the two-case system of noun declension which, as is well known, was already showing signs of breaking down in manuscripts as early as the twelfth century in Western *scripta* and, elsewhere, as of the thirteenth century.[8] In our text the subject case marker *-s* for masculine singular nouns (along with the lack of *-s* for masculine plural nouns) is used with remarkable frequency and is attested in several rhymes (e.g., ll. 34–35, 339–40), indicating that the scribe was following the author's usage. Declension of *un* (e.g., "uns chascuns," l. 1549) is even more rare.[9] Other conservative linguistic and orthographic features, ones that had virtually disappeared in all texts by the late fourteenth century, include the elision of *sa* (possessive pronoun) before feminine nouns beginning with a vowel (e.g., "s'anfence," l. 320); the maintenance of older forms of possessive adjectives and pronouns (e.g., "la soue fiole," l. 1479; "Mi deciple," l. 2221); the endings *-oyz/oiz* for second-person plural verbs in the future tense (e.g., "appartenroyz," l. 975; "seroiz," l. 1442) and *-iens* for first-person plural imperfect and present subjunctive (e.g., "aviens," l. 819; "Puissiens," l. 1341); the maintenance of vowel hiatus in most cases, sometimes with *h* as a marker (e.g., "deceü," l. 1570; "mehu," l. 249); and the maintenance of etymological first-person singular present verb forms (no addition of analogical *-e* or *-s*, except in the case of the verb *estre*, written as "suis" throughout). The state of the language is quite similar to that of the *Passion du Palatinus*, which Grace Frank posits as an early fourteenth-century reworking of a late thirteenth-century original.[10] The manuscript, which scholars now date to around 1340–1350, would support an earlier fourteenth-century date for the play based on linguistic evidence.[11]

Regarding provenance, it is difficult to localize texts written after the late thirteenth century on the basis of known dialectal traits, inasmuch as many of these traits, especially Picardisms, had been incorporated into a literary language common to many regions extending from the North to the South-Center (Burgundy) and including Ile-de-France. Nonetheless, certain of these traits (e.g., the *-oiz* and *-iens* verb endings), along with the conserva-

---

[8] See Christiane Marchello-Nizia, *Histoire de la langue française aux XIVe et XVe siècles* (Paris: Bordas, 1979), 100.

[9] Ibid., 115.

[10] See *La Passion du Palatinus*, ed. Frank, reproduced and trans. Ribard, 82. For dating see "Mystère de la Passion du Palatinus," in *Dictionnaire des lettres françaises: Le moyen âge*, rev. ed. (Paris: Fayard, 1992).

[11] In his review of Roy's edition Valois dated the text to ca. 1330 and the manuscript to ca. 1350 (685–86); more recently Alison Stones has dated the manuscript to 1340–50. We wish to thank Professor Stones for her help on dating the manuscript.

tive attitude toward noun case endings, would tend to localize the text in the North-Eastern region of France. Other features confirming the North-Eastern localization include the palatalization of -*a* before -*ge* in such rhymes as "oultraige / couchai ge" (ll. 384–85), which is found in texts extending from the North to Burgundy and Lorraine; the first-person singular future ending -*a* (e.g., "Je vous croira," l. 609), characteristic of the Eastern regions; the reduction of -*ui* to -*u* as attested at the rhyme (e.g., "destruire/cure," ll. 511–12); and the analogical *s* found in the third-person singular present subjunctive of "crist" (l. 1262). The manuscript has been housed in the Municipal Library of Besançon since the early eighteenth century, and Roy hypothesizes that it was once a part of the collection of the cardinal of Granvelle, born in Besançon in 1517, who was also bishop of Arras.[12] The linguistic evidence, along with the book's known history, therefore, suggests that the manuscript was probably transcribed in an area extending as far north as Saint-Quentin, as far east as Lorraine, and perhaps as far west as the eastern portion of Ile-de-France.

In his typology of French play manuscripts Graham A. Runnalls classifies Besançon 579 as belonging to Type G, that is, manuscripts that "were written in order to keep a record of a performed text, and were often used as gifts to patrons. They therefore follow a performance, rather than precede it."[13] Given the somewhat luxurious nature of this illuminated manuscript, it seems clear that it was not used as a script for performance, although it is not possible to determine whether there was, as Runnalls states of Type G manuscripts in general, "often a considerable lapse of time between the date of the performance and the date of the manuscript."[14]

THEOLOGICAL CONTEXTS

Christian theology understands history as teleological, as a trajectory running from the Creation of the world by God to the fulfillment of history at the end of time in Christ's judgment of all humankind, at which time the

---

[12] *Jour du Jugement*, ed. Roy, 12–13.

[13] Runnalls, "Towards a Typology," 96–113. Besançon 579 has the following characteristics of Type G manuscripts: (a) ruled pages and evenly spaced text, (b) centered stage directions, (c) few stage directions, (d) few corrections, (e) frequent ornamentation, (f) miniatures, (h) written on parchment, and (i) two-column text written on both folio sides. (See 107–8.)

[14] Ibid., 108. The apparent scribal confusion regarding the name Le Matham/Leviathan (see note to the rubric following line 353)—a confusion arising from written, rather than oral, transmission of the text—further accentuates the presentation aspect of the manuscript and the probability that it was not used for performance.

secular world will be destroyed, the evil will be punished for eternity with and by the demons in Hell, and the righteous will join God, the angels, and the saints in Heaven, the New Jerusalem. History is divided into two large segments by the Incarnation of Christ and his Crucifixion and Resurrection, a division represented by the two major sections of the Christian Bible, the Old and New Testaments. The Christian church begun by Christ and formally established at Pentecost is to be challenged by Antichrist at the end of time before the Second Coming of Christ. The importance of this understanding of history is evident throughout medieval drama, which emphasizes the representation of Creation, the Passion, and the Last Judgment. Perhaps the best-known examples of this historical trajectory are the Middle English cycle plays, all of which stage the beginning, middle, and end of salvation history, but the concern especially with the Creation and Fall, the Trial, Crucifixion, and Resurrection of Christ, and Doomsday is also evident in many medieval continental plays, such as the elaborate and often lengthy French mystères.[15]

There is a vast and continuous tradition of descriptions of, commentaries on, and warnings about the Last Judgment ranging from the earliest texts of the Christian Church throughout the Middle Ages. In the later Middle Ages the Last Judgment was especially emphasized by theologians, preachers, latter-day prophets, artists, and poets and was taught to the populace by means of sermons, poems, sculpture, stained glass, and paintings, as well as plays. In his apocalyptic discourse to his disciples (Matt. 24–25) Christ describes the frightful events of the last days, emphasizing their imminence and unexpected and sudden nature (24:34–39) and focusing on the majesty and glory of the Second Coming and the universal judgment of good and evil:

> And when the Son of man shall come in his majesty, and all the angels with him, then shall he sit upon the seat of his majesty: And all the nations shall be gathered together before him, and he shall separate them one from another, as the shepherd separateth the sheep from the goats: And he shall set the sheep on his right hand, but the goats on his left. (Matt. 25:31–33)

This passage, along with several descriptions of the Day of the Lord in the Hebrew Bible, provides the basis of medieval expectations regarding the last days and the biblical source of much of the action of the concluding scenes in the *Jour du Jugement*. The other major source for the play's treatment of

---

[15] The most comprehensive study of the French mystères remains Petit de Julleville's *Histoire du théâtre en France*; see also Roy's *Le Mystère de la passion en France*. For the English cycles see Stevens, *Four Middle English Mystery Cycles*.

the Last Judgment and the events leading to it is the last book of the New Testament, the Apocalypse of John or Book of Revelation. Its highly visual, esoteric, and often violent imagery, for example, lies behind the representation of the vials of wrath (Apoc. 16) poured out by the angels onto the evil followers of Antichrist.

Related to Doomsday in medieval eschatology are a series of expectations ranging from the attack of Antichrist to the cosmic signs of the end. Augustine outlines the major events expected to take place in the last days in his *City of God*, the text that formed the authoritative foundation of the Christian philosophy of history:

> There is no one therefore who denies or doubts that the last judgement, as it is foretold in holy Scripture, is to be executed by Jesus Christ, unless it is someone who, with an unbelievable kind of animosity or blindness, does not believe in those sacred writings, which have by now demonstrated their truth to the whole world. And so in that judgement, or in connection with that judgement, we have learnt that those events are to come about: Elijah the Tishbite will come; Jews will accept the faith; Antichrist will persecute; Christ will judge; the dead will rise again; the good and the evil will be separated; the earth will be destroyed in the flames and then will be renewed.[16]

As is evident in Augustine's quick overview, the expectation that Antichrist will appear shortly before the Last Judgment to challenge the Christian Church, deceiving even the elect and persecuting those who remain faithful, is a central tenet of medieval Christian eschatology.[17] The Bible does not develop in any detail the expectations concerning Antichrist—the name is mentioned only in the first two epistles of John. Nevertheless, exegetes interpreted a series of Old and New Testament passages describing various figures of evil (e.g., the "little horn," Dan. 7:8; the "false Christs and false prophets," Matt. 24:24; and the "son of perdition," 2 Thess. 2:3), opponents and persecutors of the early Church (e.g., Herod, Simon Magus, and Nero), and strange and terrifying creatures (e.g., the several beasts described in the Book of Daniel and the Apocalypse) as linked and as providing clues for the initiated to decipher the characteristics of the final figure of evil. Throughout a wide range of medieval biblical commentary these passages came to be understood as describing types and symbols of Antichrist that served as prophetic warnings of his career in the last days.[18]

---

[16] Augustine, *City of God*, 20.30, trans. Bettenson, ed. Knowles, 963.

[17] For the tradition in the Middle Ages see Emmerson, *Antichrist in the Middle Ages*; and McGinn, *Antichrist*, 79–199.

[18] On the types and symbols of Antichrist in medieval exegesis see Emmerson,

The legend of Antichrist was first fully described by a tenth-century French abbot, Adso of Montier-en-Der, in his *Libellus de Antichristo* (ca. 954), a book composed for the French Queen Gerberga.[19] It developed a vita or life of Antichrist, modeled on a form well known from contemporary saints lives.[20] Describing Antichrist's birth, career of deceit and tyranny, the opposition of Enoch and Elijah, and Antichrist's death, it presented a coherent account of this final opponent that could be easily integrated into sermons, poems, and plays and that could provide the narrative basis for artistic representations of Antichrist's life. Thus, several years before the composition of the *Jour du Jugement*, which was clearly influenced by Adso's *Libellus*, the figure of Antichrist was well established in French literature in such works as Berengier's *De l'avenement Antecrist* (early thirteenth century), Huon de Méry's *Tournoiement de l'Antecrist* (ca. 1234–1237), and Geufroi de Paris's *Bibles des sept états du monde* (ca. 1243).[21]

ANTICHRIST AND DOOMSDAY
IN MEDIEVAL DRAMA

Although the *Jour du Jugement* is unique as the only single extant medieval play giving full dramatic treatment to both the legend of Antichrist and the Last Judgment, other medieval plays develop and link the two eschatological expectations. The fourteenth-century Doomsday play from Perugia, for example, includes a ninety-six-line introduction detailing the career of Antichrist before it stages the Last Judgment.[22] More fully developed are the three plays that conclude the sixteenth-century Chester Cycle, "The Prophets of Antichrist" (play 22), "Antichrist" (play 23), and "The Last Judgment" (play 24).[23] The "Prophets," and in fact all the earlier plays in this late

---

Antichrist in the Middle Ages, 21–49.

[19] Adso of Montier-en-Der, *Libellus de Antichristo*. It is available in two translations: by McGinn, in *Apocalyptic Spirituality*, 81–96; and by Wright, in his translation of the *Ludus de Antichristo, Play of Antichrist*, 100–10.

[20] See Emmerson, "Antichrist as Anti-Saint: The Significance of Abbot Adso's *Libellus de Antichristo*," *American Benedictine Review* 30 (1979): 175–90.

[21] For Berengier see *Deux versions inédites de la légende de l'Antechrist en vers français du xiii* siècle*, ed. E. Walberg (Lund: C. W. K. Gleerup, 1928). For Huon de Méry see *Li Tornoiemenz Antecrit*, ed. Georg Wimmer, Ausgaben und Abhandlungen aus dem Gebiete der romanischen Philologie, 76 (Marburg, 1888); and Emmerson, *Antichrist in the Middle Ages*, 188–93. For Geufroi de Paris see L. E. Kastner, "Some Old French Poems on the Antichrist," *Modern Language Review* 2 (1906–07): 26–31.

[22] For an edition see *Perugia Last Judgment Play*, ed. de Bartholomaeis, 1:35–52. See also Emmerson, *Antichrist in the Middle Ages*, 164–65; and Aichele, *Antichristdrama*, 34–35.

[23] For an edition see *The Chester Mystery Cycle*, ed. Lumiansky and Mills, 396–463;

Middle English cycle, summarize salvation history dramatically, serving a purpose similar to that of the Preacher's introductory sermon in the *Jour du Jugement*. The next two plays, "Antichrist" and "Last Judgment," then dramatize the eschatological concerns of the *Jour du Jugement*, although, since the two themes are represented in separate pageants, they are not linked as closely as they are within our single play.[24] The two treatments differ in other ways as well. The Chester Cycle does not stage the entire life of Antichrist from birth to death, as does the *Jour du Jugement*, but instead focuses on his career of deceit, on his conversion of four representative kings, and especially on his dispute with Enoch and Elijah. Perhaps the most significant difference is that Chester does not represent the Jews as followers of Antichrist.

In contrast, the Künzelsau Corpus Christi Cycle (ca. 1479), which, like the *Jour du Jugement*, has a strong anti-Semitic slant, emphasizes Antichrist's Jewish supporters.[25] This cycle is interesting because the eschatological themes are introduced by the Parable of the Five Wise and Foolish Virgins (Matt. 25:1–13), an important component of Christ's apocalyptic warnings and the subject of the earliest eschatological play, the late eleventh-century *Sponsus*.[26] The three-day mystère performed at Modane in 1580 and 1606 is the most elaborate of the plays combining Antichrist and the Last Judgment. Its action requires 114 actors for the first day, 138 for the second, and an amazing 160 for the third day.[27] Although only a partial text is extant, we know that, like the *Jour du Jugement*, the Modane play staged the full life of Antichrist, from his birth to his death, which in Modane takes place when he attempts to ascend to Heaven. Unlike the *Jour du Jugement*, which gives roughly equal attention to Antichrist and Doomsday, the Modane play concentrates on Antichrist, devoting its first two days and much of the third to the career of the final deceiver. Much simpler is the similarly late Chur *Last Judgment* play, which again uses the legend of Antichrist to introduce Doomsday. A particularly interesting feature of this play is that, along with the usual Jewish followers of Antichrist, it includes personifications of the

---

for a study see Emmerson, *Antichrist in the Middle Ages*, 180–87.

[24] On the relation between the Chester "Antichrist" and "Last Judgment," see Emmerson, " 'Nowe Ys Common This Daye,' " 89–120.

[25] For an edition see *Das Künzelsauer Fronleichnamspiel*, ed. Liebenow. For discussion see Emmerson, *Antichrist in the Middle Ages*, 165; and Aichele, *Antichristdrama*, 45–48.

[26] For an edition see *Sponsus: Dramma delle Vergine Prudenti e delle Vergine Stolte*, ed. Raffaello Monterosso and D'Arco Silvio Avalle (Milan: Riccardo Ricciardi, 1965); for a study see Sheingorn, " 'For God Is Such a Doomsman,' " 31–36.

[27] See *Le Mystère de l'Antéchrist et du Jugement de Dieu*, ed. Gros, 13–19; Gros edits a lengthy fragment of the first day's text, 49–154. See also Chocheyras, *Le Théâtre religieux en Savoie au 16ᵉ siècle*, 20–28 and 181–224; and Aichele, *Antichristdrama*, 93–100.

deadly sins.[28]

In addition to these plays that link Antichrist to the Last Judgment, some medieval plays focus only on Antichrist's final assault on the Church. The first and most important of these is the twelfth-century *Ludus de Antichristo*, a Latin play from the abbey of Tegernsee, in Bavaria.[29] Like the *Jour du Jugement* it draws from the tradition of Adso's *Libellus*, but its treatment of Antichrist is highly circumscribed and placed within the tradition of the Last World Emperor, the expectation that just before the end of time one Christian ruler will reunite Christendom and subjugate the enemies of Christianity in preparation for the Second Coming. Early in the *Ludus de Antichristo* the Emperor establishes political control of the world, but after he gives up his crown on the Mount of Olives in a gesture of humility and homage to Christ, Antichrist appears, accompanied by Hypocrisy and Heresy. Through deceit and violence they gradually gain control of the world, despite the preaching of Enoch and Elijah. The play concludes optimistically, though: after a sudden *deus ex machina* Antichrist is defeated and those who have been deceived rejoin Ecclesia. This concern with the role of the emperor characterizes other Germanic eschatological plays. For example, *Des Entkrist Vasnacht*, a Swiss play probably dating to the middle of the fourteenth century, also emphasizes the role of the Emperor.[30] It also stages the Jewish supporters of Antichrist, the opposition of Enoch and Elijah, and the four means by which he gains power, through false teaching, miraculous deeds, bribery, and persecution of the faithful. These features, in fact, typify most Antichrist drama.[31]

Even more medieval plays stage the Last Judgment, which, as the act in which salvation history culminates, became the obvious conclusion to plays representing the Christian view of history. Perhaps the most important for comparison with the *Jour du Jugement* is the Provençal *Jutgamen General*, a fifteenth-century play concluding a dramatic cycle that began with the Creation of Adam and Eve.[32] Its 2,733 lines, roughly the length of the *Jour*

---

[28] *Churer Weltgerichtsspiel*, ed. Schulze, 89–95, lines 1366–1545.

[29] Trans. Wright under the title *The Play of Antichrist*. For studies see Emmerson, *Antichrist in the Middle Ages*, 166–72; Aichele, *Antichristdrama*, 27–33; and McGinn, *Antichrist*, 133–35.

[30] For an edition see *Des Entkrist Vasnacht*, ed. Christ-Kutter, 30–61; for a summary see Aichele, *Antichristdrama*, 40–42.

[31] Although not a large genre, there are several other plays that stage the legend of Antichrist. Aichele, *Antichristdrama*, describes or lists references to seventeen medieval, twelve Reformation, and fourteen Counter-Reformation Antichrist plays.

[32] For an edition and translation into Modern French, see *Le Jugement Dernier (Lo Jutgamen General)*, ed. Lazar; on the Provençal cycle see page 15. Although the manuscript is from the end of the fifteenth century, Lazar thinks the play dates to ca. 1440.

du Jugement, focus solely on the Last Judgment, elaborating at some length on the judgment and punishment of the Jews. It provides a very helpful opening rubric that details the play's staging, as does the Last Judgment play in the sixteenth-century Majorca Codex.[33] A German play focusing on Doomsday but also not staging the legend of Antichrist is the Augsburg *Buch vom Jüngsten Gericht*, which, like the *Jour du Jugement*, includes illustrations in its manuscript.[34] Although of the four cycles of Middle English "mystery" plays only Chester includes a play staging the legend of Antichrist, the other three cycles—the N-Town, Towneley, and York cycles—also conclude with a pageant portraying Doomsday.[35] In giving full and equal treatment to both the legend of Antichrist and the Last Judgment, the *Jour du Jugement* is unique; nevertheless, its subject matter is an important part of medieval drama and would have been well known to medieval audiences.

STAGING

No record refers to a performance of the *Jour du Jugement* in the Middle Ages, nor, to our knowledge, has there been a modern revival of the play. This situation is unfortunate, because the play is dramatically powerful, is filled with spectacle, and should be highly stageworthy. Since the manuscript includes only three stage directions, any attempt to stage the play must be based largely on interpretation of clues drawn from its dialogue and action, although the miniatures that accompany the text in the manuscript may also provide some visual evidence of how particular scenes were staged. The commentary following the translation attempts to identify the characters involved in various incidents and otherwise to clarify scenes that may not be immediately evident from the text; it also occasionally speculates on ways in which particular scenes may have been staged, sometimes drawing upon the miniatures for ideas.

This introduction will focus on larger issues of staging. Unlike several other medieval plays, including some dealing with Antichrist and Doomsday, the *Jour du Jugement* manuscript does not provide an introductory discussion of the stage plan.[36] We therefore cannot suggest with any cer-

---

[33] For translations of both rubrics see Meredith and Tailby, eds., *The Staging of Religious Drama*, 87–89.

[34] *Berliner Weltgerichtsspiel*, ed. Schulze. On other German plays see Ingebord Henderson, "German Last Judgment Plays: The State of Research," *Fifteenth-Century Studies* 14 (1988): 95–103.

[35] On these plays see Sheingorn and Bevington, "'Alle This Was Token Domysday to Drede,'" 121–45; and Leigh, "The Doomsday Mystery Play," 211–33.

[36] See the entries describing playing areas and individual locations and sets in

tainty how these eschatological subjects were staged or even where they were staged: indoors, at the crossing of a church or in a dining hall, for example; or outdoors, before the façade of a church or of another building, in a town plaza, or even in the round.[37] We are instead limited to determining staging requirements based on the action of the play and to suggesting some ways in which these requirements may have been met based on what we know about the staging of other medieval plays.

The play requires at least three large generalized playing spaces to represent the action that takes place in Heaven and Hell as well as on Earth. These spaces may be represented in two symbolic ways: vertically and horizontally. A vertically designed stage stresses the cosmic significance of the action by visualizing in traditional iconographic ways the hierarchical structure of the Christian conception of the universe, placing Christ, Mary, the angels, and the saints in Heaven; the devils in Hell; and Antichrist, his supporters, and his opponents on "middle earth" in between Heaven and Hell. If the stage is conceived in this hierarchical manner, the action of the play would unfold on three levels, perhaps on a stage similar to that described for the Last Judgment play in the Majorca Codex:

> To perform this play there shall be constructed as large a scaffold (*cadefal*) as possible in the chapel (*capella*) in the middle of the church in such a way that it juts out a bit, and immediately behind it there shall be set up another so that one can climb from one to the other.... On the lower scaffold there will be nothing. Below the scaffold, if possible, there is to be made a Hell-mouth (*una boca de infern*). If this cannot be done, a curtain (*una cortina*) is to be hung there to cover the lower part of the scaffold. That space will be Hell.[38]

The three levels of the Majorca stage are established by two scaffolds: a smaller one, representing Heaven, which is placed upon a larger lower scaffold, representing Earth. The larger scaffold is built on the church floor, which symbolically becomes the level of Hell. The interior of Hell is probably created by either the Hell-mouth[39] or a curtain covering the front of the

---

Meredith and Tailby, eds., *Staging of Religious Drama*, 71–100. See also the staging descriptions in the *Ludus de Antichristo*, trans. Wright, 67; and *Le Jugement Dernier (Lo Jutgamen General)*, ed. Lazar, 59.

[37] For French theatre-in-the-round, especially in the later Middle Ages, see Rey-Flaud, *Le Cercle magique*.

[38] Translation by Margaret Sleeman in Meredith and Tailby, eds., *Staging of Religious Drama*, 88. For the Majorca Codex, a late sixteenth-century manuscript, see ibid., 25.

[39] On the iconography of Hell Mouth see Sheingorn, " 'Who Can Open the Doors of His Face?' " 1–19.

lower scaffold, from which devils emit for their diableries, perhaps including forays into the audience. A similar, but more elaborate, version of a vertically conceived stage has been proposed for *Lo Jutgamen General*.[40]

If the *Jour du Jugement* was enacted on a tri-level stage similar to that described for the Majorca Last Judgment, the action set in Heaven would take place on the upper, smaller scaffold. This design would place the throne of Christ, probably raised somewhat on a small platform, in the center of Heaven, whence Christ would witness all the action of the play preceding Doomsday and whence he would choreograph the Last Judgment. The thrones of Mary and the Saints would be placed somewhat lower on each side, Mary and John sitting directly next to Christ. The Angels, who perhaps stand as an army poised for action, would probably flank the Saints on the far sides of the scaffold. The beauty and formality of Heaven would probably be made evident by the use of "fine purple cloths, rich curtains," and similar luxuries that we know were used to decorate stage Heavens in other plays.[41] It is possible that during the first part of the play the throne of Christ would be hidden behind a curtain, which would later be opened when the judgment scenes began, but in many medieval plays God or Christ witness the action throughout, even when they do not speak during much of the play.

Actors playing the heavenly figures on this upper scaffold would probably pose in a formal, hieratic fashion. Throughout much of the play, until the section staging the Signs of the End, they would remain relatively static to represent the timelessness of Heaven and to distinguish them from the dancing, hectic rushing to-and-fro, and slapstick of the devils in Hell. The exception to this static composition are the angels, who move to the lower scaffold to summon Enoch and Elijah from the Earthly Paradise and again to resurrect them and bring them to Heaven. It is possible that wires may have been employed to allow the angels to "fly" from one level to another.[42] Once the plot moves beyond Antichrist's career to the Signs of the End, much more action takes place on this upper scaffold, beginning with the distribution of the vials of wrath to the Angels. This shift in the locus of the action suggests that the end of time has arrived and that the opportunity for humans to choose between Heaven and Hell has passed. The Saints now ask Mary for intercession, Mary speaks directly to her Son, Christ directs the Evangelists to resurrect the dead, and the Last Judgment

---

[40] See the discussion and diagram in *Le Jugement Dernier (Lo Jutgamen General)*, ed. Lazar, 35–37.

[41] See the Prades Assumption Play in Meridith and Tailby, eds., *Staging of Religious Drama*, 79; see also 87, 92, 130.

[42] *Baptism and Temptation of Christ*, ed. Elliott and Runnalls, 18, notes that wires were used to allow angels to fly between scaffolds in the *Valenciennes Passion* of 1547.

follows.

The action set in Hell, of course, would take place on the level of the church floor or, if the play were performed outside, on the street. The devils would presumably be hidden in Hell underneath the large scaffold during the Preacher's introductory sermon and then would pour out of Hell Mouth to act out their conspiratorial parliament, to dance for joy at the birth of Antichrist, and to capture the damned and bring them back to Hell during the judgment scenes. It is possible that Hell Mouth may have been designed to open and close mechanically, as was the case in other medieval plays.[43] The scene in which Rapillart, carrying the Queen, demands, "Princes of Hell, open your doors!" (l. 2382), would take place just outside Hell Mouth; Belial and Hazart would probably first answer Rapillart from within and then come out to complain about their loss of souls. Thus, although much action takes place on the level of Hell, in this stage design very little action would be set directly inside of Hell, that is, underneath the large scaffold. Like many other plays that deal with Hell, the *Jour du Jugement* does not enact the punishments within Hell but instead briefly describes them, when, for example, the devils anticipate the suffering of the damned as they carry them to Hell (ll. 2081–85).[44]

Most of the action in the *Jour du Jugement*, however, would take place on the larger scaffold representing Earth. It is likely that the horizontal plane of this scaffold would also carry symbolic value. Its center, for example, might include a pulpit facing the audience, from which the Preacher, Enoch and Elijah, Antichrist, and Pluto would directly address the audience, who thereby function as the Christians of the last days who must decide whether or not to follow Antichrist. It is also in the center of this scaffold representing earth where the antagonists often meet, where the conflict of good and evil is acted out, and where the audience is implicitly placed and asked to decide how they will respond as Christians caught in the midst of this conflict.

The other action on this lower scaffold would as far as possible draw attention to the traditional symbolic distinction between right and left, which is always defined from the perspective of Christ sitting in judgment and is based on the division of the saved and damned at Doomsday: "And he shall

---

[43] The Metz Passion Play of 1437 included "a device (*engin*)" that allowed Hell Mouth to open and close "of its own accord when the devils wanted to go in or come out of it. And this great head (*hure*) had two great steel eyes which glittered wonderfully." Translation by Lynette R. Muir in Meredith and Tailby, eds, *Staging of Religious Drama*, 90.

[44] See Foxton, "Hell and the Devil," 71–75. Foxton (77) notes that the cauldron is the most often represented property of Hell; interestingly, it is mentioned in the *Jour du Jugement* by Hazart (l. 2083).

set the sheep on his right hand, but the goats on his left" (Matt. 25:33). Christ, seated on his throne on the upper scaffold, looks down not only on the action taking place on the lower scaffold, but also onto the audience, whom he faces directly, so that his right is the audience's left, whereas his left is the audience's right. This divine perspective means that those settings suggesting evil action would probably take place on the right side of the stage as it is faced by the audience, whereas those suggesting good action would take place on the left side. For example, the stage would probably include two gardens: the garden in Babylon, a symbolic "garden of earthly delights" where Engignart seduces Antichrist's mother, would be located on the audience's right; the second garden, representing the Earthly Paradise whence the angels summon Enoch and Elijah, would be on the audience's left.[45] The stage would also probably portray two architectural structures symbolizing good and evil: a mansion built on the audience's right, near the Babylonian garden, would contain Antichrist's throne, whereas some structure representing the true Church would be built to the left, probably near the Earthly Paradise. It would serve as the locus of the Pope and Cardinals.

Much of the play's action involves movement between the moral poles represented by these locations on the right and left. The henchmen of Antichrist, for example, would come from his throne to the church to arrest the Pope and Cardinals, taking them back to Antichrist's palace, which, along with a throne must also contain a cell where the Pope is imprisoned (l. 1373). Earlier, the Evil Bishop would probably leave the same church and move across stage to join Antichrist; then, together, they may move to the center of the stage, where the grave of the body to be falsely resurrected by Antichrist would probably be located. Setting the graves of the dead in the center of this scaffold is appropriate, because the dead are, for the time being, at least, morally neutral. It also places the dead directly below Christ's throne, so that when they are resurrected during the Last Judgment, their separation into the saved on Christ's right and the damned on Christ's left will be clearly evident to the audience.

Another structure may be set in the middle of the stage, halfway between the throne of Antichrist and the church and near the graves. When the Resurrected Body leaves Antichrist and the Evil Bishop, he states, "I am going back within the ramparts / to see my neighbors from the city" (ll. 822–23), which suggests that the stage includes a walled city, as is illustrated in miniature 32. Its gate may be very near the graves. The city is probably the locus of the Ten Kings, since they see the Resurrected Body after he enters the city (ll. 833–35). It is also probably the place whence the Blind

---

[45] Although the text does not identify either garden, the miniatures represent both actions as taking place in gardens.

Man, Leper, and the Four Poor Men come, moving across stage to Antichrist, seated at his throne. It is more difficult to determine the locus of the Jews. Although there is no reference to a synagogue or another structure specifically linked to the Jews, they are clearly connected to Babylon, since Antichrist's mother is Jewish. Considering the play's negative portrayal of the Jews, they are probably always located to Christ's left and thus firmly linked to Antichrist.

The action involving Enoch and Elijah exemplifies the flexibility of movement possible on this tri-level stage. After being called from the Earthly Paradise, they move to the center of the stage to preach at the pulpit. They probably then move back to Christ's right, but this time to the church, where, although they speak no lines, they continue to "preach" until spotted by Vivans, Marquim, and Corbadas. Medieval French plays often represent such simultaneous action.[46] The two prophets are then taken across the stage by two knights, where they confront Antichrist, debate him, and are then attacked. After Antichrist condemns them to death, Malaquim states, "we will lead them directly to their punishment" (l. 1175), suggesting that the two prophets are now led away, probably to the center of the stage, where they are killed. After they are resurrected by two angels, they "Enter that perpetual joy / which will never come to an end" (ll. 1422–23), moving upward into Heaven. They are led there by the angels, climbing steps or perhaps being lifted up in a cloud as is specified for the Modane Antichrist play.[47]

Other movement between the levels would take place when the devils come from Hell to seduce Antichrist's mother in Babylon or when they carry the damned to Hell. Angels similarly move between levels, coming down from heaven not only to summon and resurrect Enoch and Elijah, but also to pour out the vials of wrath onto the damned. Although John the Evangelist clearly speaks from the upper scaffold when he invites the angels to take the vials of wrath, along with the other evangelists he comes down from Heaven to resurrect the dead. God directs the Four Evangelists to "get up without any further delay" (l. 1879), suggesting that they have been seated on thrones in Heaven; they then go to the four corners of the earth, perhaps surrounding the tombs in the center of the stage. It is possible that the resurrected dead respond to the evangelists by coming up from beneath the scaffold through trap doors.[48]

---

[46] Elliott and Runnalls note in *Baptism and Temptation of Christ* that "simultaneous, interlocking action is characteristic of the structural technique of French Passion plays in general" (16).

[47] The Modane records state: "Then they shall cunningly and skillfully make the cloud to raise up Elijah and Enoch to Paradise." Translation by Muir in Meredith and Tailby, eds., *The Staging of Religious Drama*, 106.

[48] A fifteenth-century Resurrection play from Paris, for example, shows how a

So far we have focused on a stage designed to emphasize the vertical nature of the Christian understanding of the universe as divided into Heaven, Earth, and Hell. The second way to conceive the staging of the *Jour du Jugement* is in a horizontal fashion, as "a series of scaffolds or 'mansions' representing specific locales, arranged about a central unlocalized playing-area or 'place.'"[49] Each scaffold is the locus of a character or a group of related characters who speak at various points during the play. Often the action takes place in an undefined *platea* or place, where characters meet as they move from one scaffold to another. A well designed stage plan will establish a symbolic relationship between the scaffolds, so that as the play unfolds and characters move from one scaffold to another, the movement symbolically underscores the dialogue and action of the play. Such a plan is envisioned, for example, in the *Ludus de Antichristo*, which in its introduction describes a series of *sedes* or seats, each associated with one of the major players in the eschatological drama:

> Scene: The Temple of the Lord and seven royal seats arranged in the following manner: to the east the Temple of the Lord; around it are arranged the seat of the King of Jerusalem and the seat of Synagoga. To the west the seat of the Emperor of the Romans; around it are arranged the seat of the King of the Teutons and the seat of the King of the Franks. To the south the seat of the King of the Greeks. To the south the seat of the King of Babylonia and of Gentilitas.[50]

This description leaves many questions unanswered, but it is clear that the stage plan imagines the action as covering the entire world and represents the action in geographic terms from the perspective of its twelfth-century German audience. The plan works reasonably well for the *Ludus de Antichristo*, since its action often portrays political struggle between various kings, involves disputes over territories, and is essentially limited to events on earth.

The extent to which a similarly conceived plan would be suitable for the

---

trap door could be used to represent a resurrection: "And Jesus...shall cunningly (*subtillement*) and suddenly rise up from the tomb through a wooden trapdoor (*trappe de boys colleysse*) which will close itself again as soon as he has risen." Translation by Muir, in Meredith and Tailby, eds., *The Staging of Religious Drama*, 97. Lazar's stage diagram for *Le Jugement Dernier (Lo Jutgamen General)* (37) imagines the tombs of the resurrected as openings in the primary scaffold.

[49] Elliott and Runnalls, eds, *Baptism and Temptation of Christ*, 17. They argue that the "mansion and place" format is the most common method of staging medieval French religious plays.

[50] *Ludus de Antichristo*, trans. Wright under the title *Play of Antichrist*, 67; for a discussion of staging see 52–56.

Jour du Jugement, with its action set in Heaven and Hell as well as on Earth, is worth considering. In the *Ludus de Antichristo* plan, the placement of the Temple and Jerusalem to the east represents not only its geographic position but also its symbolic status, since the east is traditionally morally privileged. Thus the east may be associated with Heaven, as it is in the plans for the sixteenth-century Lucerne Easter play, which locates Heaven to the east and Hell to the west.[51] The famous drawing for *The Castle of Perseverance*, a fifteenth-century Middle English morality play, similarly attaches symbolic value to geographical position.[52] It places the scaffold of God in the east, of World in the west, and of Belial in the north, a location traditionally associated with the devil.

If a horizontally designed stage with symbolic associations is planned for the *Jour du Jugement*, scaffolds would be needed for Heaven, which would include the thrones of Christ, Mary, and the Saints as well as places for the Angels; for Hell, where the parliament of Devils and their exuberant dance would be set; for Antichrist's palace, which would include his throne and the prison cell; for Babylon, where Antichrist would be conceived and born and perhaps where the Jews would find their home; for the walled city of the Ten Kings and those benefiting from Antichrist's false miracles; for the Earthly Paradise; and for the church, where the Bishop, Pope, and Cardinals reside. As much as possible the location of these scaffolds should develop symbolic associations, with Heaven being located to the east, Hell opposite Heaven to the west, and Antichrist's throne established to the north. The other scaffolds would be arranged between or near these three crucial locations, the Earthly Paradise and the church, for example, being located in the east near Heaven, whereas Babylon would be placed near Antichrist in the north. Perhaps the pulpit would appropriately be placed in the south, directly before the audience and in front of the tombs from which the dead are resurrected.

The movement of actors in this staging plan would in one sense be similar to that of the vertical staging plan, with much of the action taking place in the undefined *platea*, probably near the audience. There are three important differences between the two types of plans, however. First, there would be more movement in the horizontal than in the vertical plan, since characters would often need to move down from one scaffold, across the *platea*, and up another scaffold. Second, the symbolic value of vertical movement would be largely lost, since climbing the scaffold of God would

---

[51] For a diagram of the plans see the inside back cover of Meredith and Tailby, eds., *Staging of Religious Drama*; see also the description on 81–87.

[52] For the diagram see Clifford Davidson, *Illustrations of the Stage and Acting in England to 1580*, Early Drama, Art, and Music Monograph Series, 16 (Kalamazoo: Medieval Institute Publications, 1991), fig. 55.

not be essentially different from climbing the scaffold of Hell. The third and most significant difference is the loss of the iconographic associations of right and left, which are so crucial to the vertical plan. What is gained in the horizontal plan, however, is a much larger playing space, since the tri-level vertical stage could be very crowded for the huge cast of the *Jour du Jugement*. Because Hell would be represented by its own scaffold, furthermore, it probably would be easier to represent more action within Hell, such as the parliament and dance of the Devils.

Whatever staging plan is imagined for the *Jour du Jugement*, it is clear that the dialogue and action of the play require certain stage properties. The importance of the pulpit has already been mentioned, as have the thrones of God, Mary, the Saints, and Antichrist.[53] The Earthly Paradise may have been furnished with trees as is evident in miniature 16 and described for other plays.[54] Babylon, whether or not it includes a garden, requires a bed for the representation of both the conception and birth of Antichrist, as is pictured in miniatures 6 and 12. Its architecture may be "orientalized" or perhaps furnished to suggest a synagogue. Among the numerous objects mentioned in the play are the coins that are minted to establish Antichrist's control, the scroll from which Pluto reads Antichrist's proclamation, the vials of wrath poured out by the Angels, the trumpets blown by the Four Evangelists to resurrect the dead, and the lance and cross that the angels display during the judgment scenes. Although not mentioned in the play, it is possible that the Saints carried or wore their various attributes. The illustrations in the manuscript of the Augsburg *Buch vom Jüngsten Gericht*, for example, show the saints holding their attributes.[55]

If the *Jour du Jugement* followed the conventions of other medieval plays for which we have more information, it is likely that much attention was given to costuming. Christ would probably be dressed in a robe that could be opened to show his wounds, perhaps a red robe as pictured in several of the manuscript's miniatures. Mary probably would wear a blue outer robe, as is typical of medieval iconography and as is shown in miniatures 71–74;

---

[53] *Lo Jutgamen General*, ed. Lazar, calls for "well-adorned" thrones for both Christ and Mary; the saints are to be "arranged on benches." See Meredith and Tailby, eds., *Staging of Religious Drama*, 87. Descriptions of sometimes elaborate thrones are among the most common stage properties in medieval plays.

[54] The Paris Resurrection play requires that on the inside of the Earthly Paradise "be trees, some in blossom, others laden with fruit of different kinds such as cherries, plums, apples, pears, almonds, oranges, figs, pomegranates, and grapes.... And they should be of such a height as to be visible above the wall all over the playing area." Translation by Muir, ibid., 92–93.

[55] *Berliner Weltgerichtsspiel*, ed. Schulze, fols. 37^r–39^v. Also noteworthy are the records of the Barcelona Corpus Christi procession (1424), which provide a long list of attributes for the saints; see Meredith and Tailby, *Staging of Religious Drama*, 127–29.

in the Lucerne directions, for example, her costume is "a white underskirt or nun's skirt and over it a blue silk coat," and she is to be given "a beautiful spread-out woman's hairstyle with a halo (*schyn*) above it, white hose and shoes, honorable."[56] The miniatures represent the Angels in white and as winged and picture the two prophets as bearded and bald and in simple white robes. The Jews would probably wear lavish robes and pointed hats, the Jews hat that is often portrayed in medieval art and is evident in the manuscript's miniatures.[57] The Bishop, Pope, and Cardinals are shown with the signs of their office, which is probably how they were costumed in the play; the Fourth Knight, for instance, refers to the Cardinals as "you with the red hoods!" (l. 1265). It is likely that the Ten Kings would be dressed splendidly in contemporary fashion, which is also how miniature 5 represents the devil Engignart when he transforms himself into a courtly lover to seduce Antichrist's Mother, who is shown costumed in scarlet. Antichrist could also be dressed in fine raiment like the Kings, although the miniatures show him, once he begins his false preaching, wearing a friar's habit. Those resurrected from the dead would probably wear some kind of body suit that made them appear as naked, which is how they are pictured in the miniatures and often represented on the medieval stage. Medieval drama usually emphasizes the grotesque nature of devils, whose appearance is often described as horrible and frightening and who sometimes wear animal skins.[58] The miniatures represent them as brownish and blackish, hairy and furry, with horns and long arms.

The *Jour du Jugement* is a play filled with spectacle, and it is likely that in production, like much other medieval drama, it depended upon a wide range of special effects. For example, Haquim notes that "the earth shook

---

[56] Translation by John Tailby, in Meredith and Tailby, eds., *Staging of Religious Drama*, 138.

[57] The Lucerne play costumed the Jews "in good Jewish style, in long clothes, or else priestly clothing inside and then outside over it capes with hoods (*guglen*), also their Jewish hats with buttons and tassels, but some flat with turned-up brims (*überlitzen*); they should have their clothing covered all over with Jewish letters." Translation by Tailby, ibid., 135.

[58] A report from Florence in 1304 describes a series of barges on the Arno that represented a "likeness of Hell, with fires and other punishments and torments, with men disguised as demons of most horrible appearance and others who appeared like people in the form of naked souls, and they were put to various tortures with very great shouting and screaming and storming; and this appeared like a most terrible and frightening thing to hear and see." Translation by Raffaella Ferrari, ibid., 67. The float for Hell in the Bourges parade (1536) describes Lucifer as follows: "He wore a bear skin with a sequin hanging from each hair and a pelt with two [animal] masks (*tymbre à deux museaux*) adorned with various colored materials; he ceaselessly vomited flames, held in his hands various serpents or vipers which moved and spat fire." Translation by Muir, ibid., 91.

most powerfully" (l. 1201) at the moment when Enoch and Elijah are murdered, and it is possible that such an earthquake was staged, as it was in the 1580 performance of the Modane Antichrist play.[59] It is fascinating to imagine how the various effects of the vials of wrath may have been staged, including rivers filled with blood (ll. 1539–40), and how God's command to "engulf" the world "in fire and flames" (l. 1867) was accomplished. We know that fires were quite common on the medieval stage and that fire was used in the Provençal *Jutgamen General* to punish the damned in Hell.[60] The atmosphere of Hell was probably represented by explosions as well as other clashing sounds, shouting, thunder, and even cannon-fire.[61] Fireworks are often associated with devils in medieval drama; the directions for the Modane Antichrist play, for example, call for fireworks "for each of the devils every time they emerge from Hell and for Lucifer each time he speaks, each day."[62] Although directions are not given for hellish music, it is likely that some music accompanied the dance of the Devils when they celebrate the conception of Antichrist.[63] In contrast the play would also probably include some form of heavenly music, in addition to the trumpets played by the Four Evangelists during the resurrection of the dead. Singing is limited to the three angelic songs, for which the manuscript provides music.[64]

---

[59] "They shall by a device (*par engin*) make an earthquake when necessary with everything possible to make it convincing (*pur lui ressembler*)." Translation by Muir, ibid., 105.

[60] "Then, in the presence of Lucifer and the others, the devils begin to turn the wheels and bring iron pitchforks and gaffs to torment the souls inside when anyone pokes his head out of the pit because of the pressure (*espenge*), and those within throw fire and smoke out of the hole when it is time to speak." Translation by Muir, ibid., 111. The Modane Antichrist notes that the "master painters have promised to serve well and truly in all things needful in the handling of fire (*en l'art du feu*)," 106. The records of the Coventry Drapers show payments for "worlds" to be set on fire during the Last Judgment pageant; see 107–9.

[61] Richard Rastall, in "Sounds of Hell," notes that "Hell is certainly a noisy place" (111). The Paris *Resurrection* (1419) describes Hell as emitting "flaming sulphur, cannon-fire, thunder, and other fearful sounds." The stage directions opening the Rouen Nativity play (1474) note that "all the devils cry out together with the drums and other thunderings made by machines (*engins*), and the cannon (*couleuvrines*) are shot off and flames of fire are thrown out from the nostrils, the eyes, and the ears [of the Hell's mouth]." Translation by Muir, in Meredith and Tailby, eds., *Staging of Religious Drama*, 90, 157.

[62] Translation by Muir, in Meredith and Tailby, eds., *Staging of Religious Drama*, 105.

[63] On dancing see Rastall, "Sounds of Hell," 119–22.

[64] See *Jour du Jugement*, ed. Roy, 14–15, the commentary on lines 456–63, 1410–17, and 2203–8, and Appendix 3 below.

THE MINIATURES

Besançon 579 includes eighty-nine miniatures: one, a full-page representation of the Last Judgment, introduces the play; and another eighty-eight are painted within the columns of the play's text. These miniatures are quite worn, which suggests that they received extensive attention from readers of the manuscript. An iconographic analysis of the miniatures is not possible in this introduction, but a brief description of each is provided in Appendix 2.

The relationship between the miniatures and the play deserves some consideration, however. Given the nature of the manuscript, it is unlikely that Besançon 579 was ever used as a working script in the theater, nor is there any way to determine if the manuscript records an actual production of the play. The miniatures follow the text quite closely and are placed within the manuscript usually in the same columns and near the text describing the scenes they picture (see the two pages from the manuscript included with this volume). The text thus probably serves as the foundation for the miniatures, although the miniatures do add important information that is not always explicit in the text itself, such as depicting which characters are present in a scene, something the text rarely specifies. It is possible that in those few instances when the miniatures depart from the text or represent the dramatic scenes with details not drawn from the text—as when, for example, the miniatures illustrate the conception of Antichrist or depict him dressed in a friar's habit—they represent the artist's memory of an actual performance. But it is also possible that in such situations the artist is following visual models rather than the costuming and staging of a dramatic production. The legend of Antichrist and the Last Judgment are both widely represented in medieval art, and iconographic models, especially for the Last Judgment, are rich and plentiful.[65] It is thus important to be cautious when using the miniatures to address questions concerning staging, although they can be quite helpful for some scenes. Brief suggestions of how the miniatures may help twentieth-century readers visualize the play are occasionally included in the commentary and notes that accompany the translation.

These beautifully executed miniatures are extremely valuable, both in their own right as works of art and as early responses to, and visual interpretations of, the *Jour du Jugement*. They deserve a full iconographic study analyzing both the literary and artistic traditions from which they draw.

---

[65] On Antichrist in medieval art see Emmerson, *Antichrist in the Middle Ages*, 108–45; McGinn, "Portraying Antichrist"; and Wright, *Art and Antichrist in Medieval Europe*. On the Last Judgment see Sheingorn, " 'For God is Such a Doomsman,' " 15–58.

A NOTE ON THE TRANSLATION

The translation is based on Émile Roy's edition, *Le Jour du Jugement: Mystère français sur le Grand Schisme*, published in 1902, which has been checked against the manuscript in Besançon. All manuscript readings in which we disagree with Roy are noted in the commentary. Following the guidelines of the Early European Drama Translation Series, the translation is in free verse approximating but not replicating the character of the original octosyllabic line. The translation is intended to be as literal as possible.

All speaker identifications and stage directions included in the translation are from the manuscript itself. No stage directions are added; instead, staging problems and suggested directions are discussed in the commentary. An open circle is used to identify a line or group of lines discussed in the commentary; ellipses identify lacunae in the manuscript. Throughout, Latin texts are set in italic type, as are French rubrics identifying speakers or providing stage directions. Line numbers, placed in the right-hand margins, have been added.

FACSIMILE PAGES

To give some indication of the design and illustration of the manuscript, we have reproduced two of its folios. Fol. 8ᵛ (ll. 430–56) indicates the spacing of the dialogues and the treatment of rubrics identifying the speakers of six different speeches. It includes two miniatures (nos. 14, 15), which represent the baby Antichrist and his mother and two devils dressed as men. It also includes a few lines of the musical notation for the angel's song calling Enoch and Elijah from the Earthly Paradise. The second facsimile page, of fol. 13ᵛ (ll. 775–810), is perhaps more typical of the manuscript; it includes fewer but longer speeches. Its two miniatures (nos. 30, 31) show Antichrist's false resurrection of the dead.

Facsimile 1 (fol. 8ᵛ), lines 430–56. Reproduced by permission of the Bibliothèque Municipale de Besançon.

Facsimile 2 (fol. 13ᵛ), lines 775–810. Reproduced by permission of the Bibliothèque Municipale de Besançon.

[The Day of Judgment]

[DRAMATIS PERSONAE]°

The devils
Satan
Beelzebub
Pluto
Engignart
Belial
Foule
Agrappart
Hazart
Le Matam
Rapillart
Antichrist
Antichrist's Mother
The Girl
First Knight
Second Knight
Third Knight
Fourth Knight
Malaquim
Mossé
Caiaphas
Vivans
Marquim
Corbadas

Haquim
Annes
The Blind Man
The Leper
First Poor Man
Second Poor Man
Third Poor Man
Fourth Poor Man
Usurer's Nurse
Usurer's Child
The Usurer
His Wife
The Lawyer
The Miser
The Bailiff
The Provost
The Abbess
The Prioress
The Bishop
The Resurrected Body
The Queen
Her Ladies
Dagobert, king
Malabrum, king

[Dramatis Personae]. Before the initial large miniature that precedes the beginning of the play, the MS (fol. 1ʳ–1ᵛ) lists ninety-four characters, but not in the order of their appearance. The first entry in the list, "Li deable" (a nominative masculine plural noun), we consider a subheading for the named devils who follow; there is no character in the play named "The Devil." One character who speaks in the play, Thaddeus (ll. 2295–2302), is not included in this introductory list. Two characters listed here do not appear in the play as extant: the Queen's Ladies ("Ses damoiselles," fol. 1ʳ) and the Rich Clerk ("Le riche clerc," fol. 1ʳ). For their possible roles, see the notes following ll. 2156 and 2370. In addition to the Angel of the Cross and the Angel of the Lance, the dramatis personae lists another eight angels, although only the First through the Seventh Angels are numbered in the play; perhaps one of the two angels who resurrect Enoch and Elijah (ll. 1410–17, 1422–23) is here distinguished as the Eighth Angel.

Ysoart, king
Fierabras, king
Accopart, king
Andoart, king
Loriquaire, king
Aroflart, king
Agoulant, king
Maillefer, king
First Cardinal
Second Cardinal
The Pope
The Good Christian
The Rich Clerk
Enoch
Elijah
Judas Maccabaeus
The Just
First Angel
Second Angel
Third Angel
Fourth Angel
Fifth Angel
Sixth Angel

Seventh Angel
Eighth Angel
Saint Peter
Saint Paul
Saint Andrew
Saint James
Saint Philip
Saint Thomas
Saint John
Saint Bartholomew
Saint Matthew
Saint Barnabas
Saint Mark
Saint Luke
Saint Simon
Saint John the Baptist
Cherubim
Seraphim
Mother of God
Angel of the Cross
Angel of the Lance
God
The Preacher

Antichrist and Judgment Day
The Middle French Jour du Jugement

Evigilabunt omnes, alii ad vitam, alii ad obprobrium.°

THE PREACHER° Calm down, fair gentle folk:
It would be neither a pleasant nor a worthy spectacle
were you to make noise here,
for on a matter of grievous consequence
for everyone, which is not only true   5
but also, for those who retain it well,
profitable to body as well as to soul—
namely the day of judgment—
I wish to deliver here to you a sermon.
Let us therefore all pray to that noble   10
Lady, dispenser of grace,°
that, through her prayer, she might make us
act upon and attend to
what I am about to say, so that we might
be able to come *in celi patria;*°   15
and then of her we shall say *Ave Maria.*°
Dies illa, dies ire.°

Evigilabunt omnes....: "All people will awaken, some to life and others to opprobrium" (Dan. 12:2). Here and throughout the manuscript, Latin texts are transcribed in red ink.

Preacher. Many medieval plays begin with a preacher or expositor providing the moral and theological background to the action and setting the scene. This function is performed by Gentilitas, Synagoga, and Ecclesia in the *Ludus de Antichristo*, but in the Chester cycle an expositor provides the background in the *Prophets of Antichrist*, commenting on the speeches of each prophet. In the *Jour du Jugement* the Preacher comes on stage and begins by quoting the Latin text, which serves as the theme or proof text for his sermon.

11 Lady: the Virgin Mary. At the Annunciation, Gabriel describes her as "full of grace" (Luke 1:28). In medieval spirituality, as *mater mediatrix*, she often intercedes on behalf of sinners who pray to her, as the kings do later in the play (ll. 1689–92).

15 *in celi patria*: into our heavenly homeland. In the Middle French this and the next three lines exemplify a feature of macaronic poetry popular in the Middle Ages, in which words in Latin and the vernacular rime: patria/Maria, ire/dire.

16 *Ave Maria*: Hail Mary (cf. Luke 1:28).

17 *Dies illa, dies ire*: "Oh Day of Wrath." A phrase often associated with the Last

Consider carefully what I am about to say.
When God first fashioned the world°
and man, pure of any sin, 20
and placed him in the Earthly Paradise,°
in that beautiful place, in that splendid realm,
and when he had created according to his design
every creature as he saw fit,
and had granted free will 25
to man, the Devil tempted°
him so quickly that he lost all his glory.
So great was the loss that, this is the truth,
we all still suffer penitence for it,
because of the sin of disobedience. 30
Because he bit into the forbidden fruit,
all our forefathers
were cast down to Hell.
The first sorrowful mother,
Eve, through whom this sin 35
was committed that has unremittingly tarnished
the entire human race,
and Adam, who at that time possessed complete
joy, could not even say where they were
as soon as they had sinned. 40
Before they became aware of their disgrace,
they were cast out of Paradise,
in the wake of God's malediction.
They then bore a progeny°
whose misdeeds were so great, 45

Judgment. Cf. Zeph. 1:15. It may here allude to the Office of the Dead or to one of the most famous hymns of the Middle Ages, Thomas of Celano's "Dies irae, dies illa." See F. J. E. Raby, ed., *The Oxford Book of Medieval Latin Verse* (Oxford: Clarendon, 1959), no. 259. A detailed description of Judgment Day, it became a sequence for the Mass of the Dead. For the music see *Liber Usualis*, 1810–13. The Preacher may sing the hymn, although the line is not set to music as are later songs in the play.

19 The preacher begins a summary of salvation history, starting with Creation and the Fall, touching on the Flood and Passion, and then emphasizing the subsequent moral decline that leads to the contemporary world and Doomsday.

21 Earthly Paradise: the Garden of Eden. According to one version of the Antichrist tradition, Enoch and Elijah await Antichrist in the Earthly Paradise.

26–43 Cf. Gen. 3:6–23. Roy, misconstruing the syntax of l. 26, suggested an emendation: "A l'omme [de] deables tampté." We prefer the MS reading and note that the playwright willingly breaks through the confines of the octosyllabic line.

44–53 Cf. Gen. 6:5–8. The evils during the days of Noah and the Flood are traditional types of the last days (cf. Matt. 24:37–39) and of the Last Judgment.

that God, because of their sins, made
them all drown in the flood.
Except Noah, whose governance he favored.
Likewise upon his children and his wife,
whom he found to be without fault,   50
he bestowed such grace that they should live on
and populate the earth,
for he considered them both virtuous and wise.
From them issued the entire human race,
which is still paying for   55
the sin of the first father.
But the price was even dearer, without doubt,
at the time when Jesus,
cloaked in our humanity,
came to battle against the king of iniquity,   60
whom he vanquished by dying
on the cross, whence, hastening,
his soul descended to Hell
and gave back to all his beloved
the heritage of Paradise   65
that they had previously lost.
Through him Death died on the cross.°
He opened to all virtuous people the portal
of Paradise,° which remains open
to the just according to their merits.   70
But the world has declined°
since that time, and is in such a state
that not a single person does good:
Everyone is following in the tracks of sin,
just as David attests,   75
for he indeed promised this impoverishment,
Dicens: "Omnes declinaverunt simul,°
inutiles facti sunt, non est qui

---

67 Death died: A commonplace of sermons and lyrics on the Passion, drawn ultimately from Hosea 13:14.

69–70 portal of Paradise: an allusion to the gates of Eden shut and guarded by angels after the expulsion of Adam and Eve (Gen. 3:24); the newly opened portal is to Heaven.

71 The increase in evil is a sign of the last days. Cf. Matt. 24:12.

77–79 Saying, "All have gone astray and become useless. There is nobody who will do good, not a single one." Ps. 13:3. Although in his edition Roy sets the Latin in four lines, they comprise three lines in the manuscript.

5

faciat bonum, non est usque ad unum.''
Now, in order for everyone to receive
this word and realize
that it is good to abandon evil
and lower oneself with humility   80
and perform good deeds in abundance,
it is my intention to disclose to you
a short passage from Holy Scripture
that provides us a frank evocation
of a certain harsh day   85
when each person, according to his merit,
will be subject to judgment
by the gentle son of God, who does not lie.
He will resuscitate the dead°
and from body and soul will create   90
through genuine resurrection°
an extraordinary spectacle.
This is the day of affliction,
marked by every bitterness and pain and
filled with tribulation,   95
mentioned by Ezekiel,°
and by the Apostle in his epistle,°
and by all Four Evangelists,°
Daniel and the other prophets,°
the holy fathers and poets.°   100
They assert that this will be a day of wrath
worse than any mouth can possibly express,
a day of shadows and darkness,

89–90 Cf. Apoc. 20:12–13.

91 The genuiness of the resurrection is emphasized to contrast with the pretended resurrections of the dead associated with the false miracles of Antichrist. Cf. ll. 756–803, 924–27, 1600–1605.

96 Cf. Ezek. 37:5–14.

97 Apostle: Paul. Cf. Rom. 14:10–12 and 2 Thes. 1:5–9.

98 Four Evangelists: three describe Doomsday in their gospels (cf. Matt. 24, Mark 13, Luke 21), and the fourth, John, describes it in the Apocalypse. Although biblical scholars now distinguish between John the revelator and the evangelist, in the Middle Ages both books were attributed to the same John, the beloved disciple.

99 Cf. Dan. 7:9–10; see also Isa. 66:15–16, Jer. 25:30–33, Joel 2:1–11 and 3:12–16, and Zeph. 1:14–18.

100 The line may allude to a famous acrostic poem describing Doomsday; attributed to the Erythean Sibyl, it is included in Augustine's *City of God*, 18.23, p. 789. See also *Jour du Jugement*, ed. Roy, 25–26.

a day of tears and of dire portent,
a dismal and very horrible day, 105
a day of misery, a painful day,
a day in which the sun and the moon°
and the stars, one by one,
will lose all their light,
and from end to end will burn° 110
all the earth and the entire universe.
No one is so untainted by sin
that he should not tremble on that day,
for at that time the private thoughts
of everyone will be displayed. 115
If a man has but a single sin,
yet will it be uncovered,
for the books will be opened that°
contain all their thoughts.
All without exception will await their sentence, 120
the good and the evil, on that day.
The true Judge on that day will
come to preside at the judgment.
He will maintain a fierce and relentless demeanor,
and, even though he is peace and concord 125
and overflowing with pity,
he will judge according to what is right.
He will look at the wicked
with an implacable countenance and say to them:
"Evil ones, never for a single day will the fire° 130
in which you are swallowed be extinguished;
go there without delay, all of you, go!"
To the virtuous he will say with affection:
"You had pity for me;°
come and join my spiritual father 135
in everlasting joy."
No one could describe to you,
nor could any heart conceive nor any mouth pronounce,
the pain that the damned will receive;

107–9 Cf. Joel 2:10 and Matt. 24:29.
110–11 Cf. Apoc. 20:9.
118–19 Cf. Apoc. 20:12.
130–32 Cf. Matt. 25:41.
134–36 Cf. Matt. 25:34.

and they will say that it was an evil hour when   140
they were born of Adam's race and born of a woman,
because they are suffering such bitter pain
that will never end at any appointed time.
Not a single relative, not a single friend°
will be able to help any other in the slightest,   145
neither through prayers nor through entreaties.
But before this most momentous day arrives,
just as Holy Scripture teaches,
there will appear in heaven and on earth
many signs as strife begins.°   150
Enoch will come with Elijah,°
just as the prophecy says,
both of whom reside in the Earthly Paradise,
and they will preach faith in the celestial King,
prohibiting anyone from believing in Antichrist—°   155
no, but rather in Jesus Christ.
For whoever believes in Antichrist
will tumble into the foul stench of Hell.
Through the world they will go off preaching
   their sermons°
and providing many good exemplary stories;   160
until Antichrist catches up with them
and puts them to death.
Three and a half days will they lie dead
and then they will make an appearance, dead,
   before everyone
in the street in the same city   165
where God was placed, in a most heinous act,

---

144 Roy amends MS "ami" to "affin" to rime with "fin" (l. 143). We prefer the MS reading.

150 MS "en mouvent guerre": the strife is possibly an allusion to "wars and rumors of wars" (Matt. 24:6), a traditional sign of the end.

151–53 The patriarch Enoch and prophet Elijah did not die. Enoch "walked with God, and was seen no more: because God took him" (Gen. 5:24; cf. Hebrews 11:5); and Elijah was taken up in a fiery chariot (2 Kings 2:11). According to tradition they await the last days in the Earthly Paradise, when, acting as the Two Witnesses (Apoc. 11:3), they will return to preach against Antichrist. See Adso, *Libellus*, 94–96. The eschatological role of Elijah is prophesied in Mal. 4:5–6. See Emmerson, *Antichrist in the Middle Ages*, 95–101.

155 This is the first time Antichrist is named. Cf. 1 John 2:18. See Emmerson, *Antichrist in the Middle Ages*, 35–37.

159–74 The details of the preaching, death, and resurrection of Enoch and Elijah are based on the prophecy of the Two Witnesses, Apoc. 11: 3–12.

8

on the cross; then they will resuscitate
and return to life.
They will be delivered from death,
just as Saint John bears witness to it   170
in his book, in the Apocalypse,
which states that from the deep abyss
will rise that fierce beast
that will inflict great harm on the world.
For almost all will believe in this beast,   175
those of the world, when they see it,
either through force, through gifts, through signs,°
until the benign King°
avenges the entire human race
upon that cruel and filthy beast,   180
who, known by the name of Antichrist,
will be cast into the pit of Hell,
along with all those of its kind.
Let us pray to God, who upholds all good things,
that he might consent to console us all   185
and sustain us in this life,
so that neither Antichrist nor another devil°
will deceive us with their lies.
Rather may we all be able with confidence
to come to the Day of Judgment,   190
without any sin, by the grace of God;

---

177 Adso (*Libellus*, 92) similarly mentions these three means by which Antichrist gains world power: force or persecution, gifts or bribes, and signs or miracles. Usually accounts of Antichrist's rule mention a fourth means, preaching or false teachings. Cf. ll. 219–21. See Emmerson, *Antichrist in the Middle Ages*, 90–92.

178–83 Cf. Apoc. 19:20.

187 Theologians usually stressed that Antichrist was not a devil, but a man possessed by the Devil. The play, however, follows a popular folkloric tradition in which Antichrist is conceived by a devil (cf. ll. 318–21) and thus is, in a sense, a devil. The most influential account, Adso's *Libellus*, suggests a middle position: "Just as the Holy Spirit came into the mother of Our Lord Jesus Christ and overshadowed her with his power and filled her with divinity so that she conceived of the Holy Spirit and what was born of her was divine and holy (Luke 1:35), so too the devil will descend into the Antichrist's mother, will completely fill her, completely encompass her, completely master her, completely possess her within and without, so that with the devil's cooperation she will conceive through a man and what will be born from her will be totally wicked, totally evil, totally lost" (*Libellus*, 90–91). Later, though, Adso adds that Antichrist is "the son of the devil, not through nature but through imitation because he will fulfill the devil's will in everything" (*Libellus*, 93). See also Emmerson, *Antichrist in the Middle Ages*, 81–83.

9

Say *Amen*, may God let it come to pass.

SATAN *first devil after the sermon*°
My friends and companions
now listen to me, all of you.
Each of us should certainly be aware   195
that we have realized a great yield,
for we have reduced the world to such a state
that there is not a single creature left pure;
all of them belong to us, man and woman,
so few are there whose lives are devoid of
    extreme disrepute.   200
We shall make all of them come to us.
God will bring about the end of the world,°
this I know, very soon.
It cannot last very long;
instead, God will judge all of us without exception   205
and he will act in our disfavor.
But before the judgment arrives,
one of us should become a man
and go straight to Babylon,°

---

after 192 Satan: leader of the devils in the play. Medieval exegesis identifies him with the dragon (Apoc. 12:9), who gives his authority to Antichrist, symbolized by the beast that rises from the sea (Apoc. 13:1–2). See Emmerson, *Antichrist in the Middle Ages,* 22–23, 39–40. On the various names and roles of the devil in medieval popular belief, see Russell, *Lucifer,* 62–91 and 245–73. For devils in medieval art and drama, see Barbara D. Palmer, "The Inhabitants of Hell," 20–40. Satan and the other seven devils in this scene come on stage together and speak in turn until all eight have had their say. A ninth devil is introduced later, after l. 353, and a tenth is introduced near the conclusion of the play, after l. 2381. They engage in a hellish parliament or council of devils, a popular scene in medieval drama; see, for example, the council called by Minos in Feo Belcari's *La Rappresentazione del Di' del Giudizio* and that called by Lucifer in Gréban's *Mystère de la Passion.* The scene in the *Jour du Jugement* was probably influenced by the hellish council that opens the prose *Merlin* attributed to Robert de Boron, author of a verse *Merlin* that has only survived in a 500-line fragment. In the prose romance the devils, furious that Jesus has come to redeem those cursed by original sin, decide to beget a child on a woman. The child, Merlin, uses the power conferred by his demonic origins for rather different purposes than does Antichrist, however. Alexandre Micha, *Merlin le prophète ou le Livre du Graal* (Paris: Editions Stock, 1980), 178ff., notes arguments that the *Merlin* was probably influenced by Adso's *Libellus,* an interesting example of the intertextuality of medieval literature. For the *Merlin* and other texts portraying a demonic conception, see *Jour du Jugement,* ed. Roy, 26–36.

202–3 Satan's speech exemplifies the prophetic powers of devils and serves to underscore the Preacher's warnings.

209 Although in some accounts Antichrist is expected to be born in Chorozaim (cf. Luke 10:13), usually his birth takes place in Babylon, "the habitation of devils" (Apoc.

making sure that, without any delay,   210
he manages to bed a woman
full of every type of disgrace,
one who has lived all her days
in a brothel, winter and summer.°
She will be of the lineage of Dan°   215
and will conceive a son.
He will call himself Antichrist
and make the people love him
through gifts, through fraudulent preaching,°
and through the resuscitation   220
of the dead, whom he will bring back to life;
even the treasures of the world will be,
in truth, completely at his disposal.

BEELZEBUB *second devil*°
This will be a very successful birth,
for I know that in all truth   225
Antichrist must of necessity
be born of a woman.°

PLUTO *third devil*°
My lords, by my soul, I strongly agree
that Engignart should perform this service.°

18:2). Adso (*Libellus*, 91) offers a compromise, stating that Antichrist is born in Babylon but reared in Bethsaida and Chorozaim. See Emmerson, *Antichrist in the Middle
Ages*, 80–81.

214 The identification of Antichrist's mother as a prostitute recalls the Whore of
Babylon (Apoc. 17), a symbol of Antichrist's false church and an opponent of the true
Church, symbolized by the Woman harassed by the dragon (Apoc. 12). It also underscores the contrast between Antichrist and Christ, who is born of the Virgin Mary,
also symbolized by the Woman of Apoc. 12.

215 Dan: here and in ll. 276, 300 we follow Roy's emendation, "de Dan" or "a Dan"
for MS "Adam." Based on Gen. 49:17 (see Adso, *Libellus*, 90), the medieval tradition
identified Dan as Antichrist's tribe. See Emmerson, *Antichrist in the Middle Ages*, 79–80.

219–21 A variation on Antichrist's means of gaining power, now including the
fourth means, fraudulent preaching. Cf. l. 177.

after 223 Beelzebub: MS "Baucibuz." Beelzebub, "the prince of the devils" (Matt.
12:24), is often identified with Satan.

227 Antichrist, born of a woman, is thus both man and devil. The notion alludes to
and inverts Christ's incarnation and birth of a woman; such inversion typifies the
tradition, in which the life of Antichrist often parodies the life of Christ. See note to
l. 187 and Emmerson, *Antichrist in the Middle Ages*, 74–76.

after 227 Although Pluto is a classical god, medieval tradition associated him with
Satan. Cf. Dante, *Inferno* 7.1–2.

229 Engignart: MS "Engingnart, Angingnars, Angingnart." Derived from the O.Fr.

11

ENGIGNART *fourth devil*

> Let anyone consider me a fool   230
> if, having undertaken this project,
> I do not carry it out in such a way
> that I am praised by you for it.

BELIAL *fifth devil*°

> I shall assist you most eagerly,
> as should all the others,   235
> so that we can bring this affair
> to its completion as soon as possible.

FOULE *sixth devil*°

> My lords, you can be completely certain
> that it is imperative to get this done,
> so no one should shrink back from it.   240
> Engignart will have what it takes to perform
>   with distinction.
> Of this, none will have any doubt.
> All this I know to be the truth.

AGRAPPART *seventh devil*°

> Fair companion, full of iniquity,
> Engignart, you will be my master;   245
> I want to be with you always,
> so as better to complete the task.
> Let us be off right now without any further delay.
> I am anxious for us to get moving.

HAZART *eighth devil*°

> My companions, you who have been chosen   250

---

engin, engignier (which is used in the prose *Merlin* to refer to devilish deception of mortals), the nominal form *engignart* had perhaps already come to refer to a devil. Its associations include deceptive, delusive, false.

after 233 Belial is a biblical name for a devil, especially one who opposes Christ (cf. 2 Cor. 6:15). See McGinn, *Antichrist*, 27–31.

after 237 Foule's name implies a crowd, multitude.

after 243 Agrappart's name may derive from Herod Agrippa; see Russell, *Lucifer*, 249. The name is given to a devil in the *Passion d'Arras* as well. The O.Fr. verb *agraper* means to grasp or to hook; the name thus suggests either greed (Covoitise in the *Roman de la Rose* is described by the related word *acrochier*) or the capture of innocent souls. Hooking probably also brings to mind visual representations of the meat hooks used by devils to torture the damned in Hell.

after 249 Hazart, who is named after a game of dice, implies hazard, risk, peril; the devil's name thus probably connotes the negative association between games of chance and evil.

to undertake this voyage,
may your entire hope
be placed in the destruction of humankind.

ENGIGNART All of you know that since my childhood
    I have been on the ready to perform evil deeds;   255
    I can see everywhere, both far and near,
    I know all people, there are no exceptions,
    not even among those who go sailing on the seas:
    It is on earth I cause all evils to occur.

SATAN Engignart, I wish to bless you   260
    on behalf of those who do not believe in God.
    Make it so that all Christians belong to us.
    Agrappart will be with you
    and he will do as much evil as he can.
    Do this without delay   265

ENGIGNART As far as this is concerned, you need not worry
    whether I will carry it out successfully...
       or do even worse things.
    My friend, let us get going right away°
    and figure out how we are to operate.

AGRAPPART My friend, do you know what we are going to do?   270
    Let us head straightway for the great city of Babylon,
    where there are to be found in abundance
    women of ill repute.

ENGIGNART Let's go! No matter whom it might please
       or displease,
    if I find a beautiful woman   275
    who is a descendant of Dan,°
    I shall shed the form of a devil
    and appear as a young man;
    so much shall I lavish in the way of gifts and
       of clever words
    that I will bring her over to my persuasion.   280
    I shall not leave her a virgin.°

---

268 With Satan's blessing Engignart and Agrappart set off for Babylon, perhaps even moving through the audience. They arrive in Babylon by l. 282.

276 Dan: cf. l. 215.

281 Since the devils seek a whore, Engignart's comment is paradoxical. He may get carried away by his boast, or perhaps the author is here assimilating Antichrist's

AGRAPPART My friend, I indeed believe that this one
   is what you are looking for.

ENGIGNART Then you must wait for me here.
   I shall cloak myself in the form of a man,°   285
   and find out everything there is to know
   about her life and her parentage.

         At this point he separates from Agrappart°

   Fair and most fortunate sister,
   sweet friend, were it to please you
   I would gladly know something about you.   290
   Are you a Christian or a Jew?

ANTICHRIST'S MOTHER
   Dear sir, whatever kind of life I lead,
   I am a Jew, and I was born°
   under the Law that God gave
   to Moses and to the rest of us;   295
   but I hate the Christians, all of them,
   those people who believe in Jesus Christ,
   for their God is insignificant,
   and I neither esteem him nor fear him in the slightest.
   Let there be no doubt, I am of the lineage of Dan;   300
   now you, tell me what you are seeking.

ENGIGNART Those are admirable words you have pronounced,
   my fair sister; it is from a foreign land
   that I have come here in search of adventure,°

---

mother to Christ's.

   285 Engignart here changes costumes. Miniature 4, placed in the MS just above these lines, shows the two near a hedge, still represented as devils, but min. 5, placed in the MS after his initial address to Antichrist's mother, shows Engignart dressed as a young man.

   after 287 A rare MS stage direction, needlessly emended by Roy. Engignart now addresses Antichrist's mother, perhaps in a garden setting as they are pictured in min. 5.

   293–300 Throughout the tradition Antichrist is born of a Jew. See Emmerson, *Antichrist in the Middle Ages*, 79. In this play, as well as in other popular versions of the life of Antichrist, his Jewish ancestry provides the basis for a strongly antisemitic bias. Antichrist's mother introduces this element here by exclaiming her hatred of Christians, which she will again stress later (ll. 390–91). For Dan, see note to l. 215.

   304 adventure: the French term, *aventure*, is used in medieval romances to designate a motivation for the protagonist's quest, which often involves a love affair. Engignart thus here compares himself to a romance hero; in the following lines he also proves to be a master of the language of *fin amours*.

and I also have come to look for a beloved.° 305
Thus I beg you, with utmost courtesy,
to agree to be my lady
and to accept me as your beloved;
grant that you will take possession of me as you would
    a lover
so that with you I may fulfill my pleasure; 310
this is what should come from love.

ANTICHRIST'S MOTHER I would consider myself a fool
if I refused such companionship;
I am very happy to be your beloved,
Do anything you want with me. 315

ENGIGNART Beauteous one, may Mohammed grant you health!°
I'm going to get to it right away.
I shall beget with you a son°
who will have tremendous power,
for, you can be sure of it, from his childhood 320
he will be proclaimed wise above all others.

ANTICHRIST'S MOTHER You truly deserve to be loved by me,
for I have learned with utmost certainty
that I have conceived a child by you.
I beg you, do not hide it from me any more, 325
tell me what your name is,
so that, if anyone asks

---

305 Roy emends the unsatisfactory "le mien" to "le mie," which makes no sense.
We suggest "amie": "Et si vien purchascier amie." This emendation is supported by
the probable repetition, "m'amie" (l. 307).

316 Although blessing a Jewish woman in the name of Mohammed makes no sense,
the prophet of Islam is often used in medieval literature as a name for a false god,
prophet, or devil. Cf. ll. 378, 413, 419, 443, 454. On the treatment of Islam in the
Antichrist tradition, see Emmerson, *Antichrist in the Middle Ages*, 67–68; and McGinn,
Antichrist, 85–87, 150–51.

318 The text does not indicate how the conception of Antichrist is staged, but
moves quickly to the mother's pregnancy (l. 324). The accompanying miniature,
placed in the MS after l. 321, shows Engignart and the woman in bed. Perhaps while
in conversation the couple are to stroll from the garden to a curtained bed, which they
occupy for a suitable period of time. The block–book *vitae Antichristi* similarly portray
the conception of Antichrist, but both parents are human and the union is incestuous.
The block books show four demons supervising the couple in bed. See Boveland, et
al., *Der Antichrist*, 3; and Emmerson, "Wynkyn de Worde's *Byrthe* and *Lyfe of Antechryst*," 290–95.

who is the father of my child,
I can reply with the truth.

ENGIGNART My sister, I am ready to disclose my name to you: 330
I am Engignart, it is no lie,
and I am one of the preeminent devils of Hell.
I shall return to see this child
I have begotten on you when he is born.
He will be named Antichrist,°   335
and will everywhere cause people to fear him.
He will destroy Christendom
and reduce it to abjection.
Provide for him when he is born
and bring him up with tenderness.   340
I am going off and herewith take my leave.°
Agrappart, our plan was a success:
I accomplished everything I had intended.

AGRAPPART Put your normal clothing back on, I beg you,°
and then we'll return to our companions   345
and all rejoice;
we really must have a great celebration over this.

ENGIGNART My lords, so long did I maintain my quest
that I did not fail to catch my prey:
I found what I was seeking.   350
I have been in Babylon,
where I won over a beloved,
with whom I did everything I desired.

---

335 Engignart's instruction for naming Antichrist parallels Gabriel's instruction for naming Jesus (cf. Luke 1:31).

341 Engignart leaves Antichrist's Mother, walking toward the hedge and the waiting Agrappart, whom he addresses in l. 342.

344 Engignart now changes back into his earlier devilish costume and returns to Hell, where he addresses the assembled devils beginning l. 348. Agrappart states that he will return as well (l. 345), but he may remain behind to watch over Antichrist's mother. In any case, he later enters with the news of Antichrist's birth (ll. 422–23).

16

LE MATAM *devil*°
> We must not keep quiet about this;
> instead we should all revel in our joy. 355

FOULE *devil*
> Not a single one of us should refrain,
> for we have all been given new life.
> From now on I will be even more prideful
> than doubtless I ever was before.

BEELZEBUB Let's all dance in one large company!° 360
> Engignart, lead this dance,
> for you are the one who impregnated that belly,
> thanks to which we are lords of the entire world.
> We have dominion over all men
> as well as over all dead men's souls. 365

ANTICHRIST'S MOTHER° Ah! demon, you might just as well
> carry me off,
> since you so thoroughly robbed me of my senses
> that you left me heavy with child!
> Now I don't know what will become of me;
> I would gladly end my life, 370
> for I don't know what else I can do.

---

after 353 Le Matam is the ninth devil in the council of Hell, suggesting an infernal parody of the nine orders of angels. His name sometimes appears as Mathan and may be related to the devil Vatan, who is called forth in *Le Jugement Dernier (Lo Jutgamen General)* (212–13, l. 2609). It is more likely, though, that Le Matam/Mathan is a scribal error for Leviatam/Leviathan, the three "jambages" of *vi* in the original transcription of the play being misread by the scribe as *m*. We owe this suggestion to Graham A. Runnalls. If the ninth devil's name is Leviatam, it would be appropriate for a play staging the life of Antichrist, since Leviathan is identified as a symbol of Antichrist from as early as Gregory's *Moralia,* as is evident in a variety of medieval art and literature. The *Liber floridus,* for example, a spiritual encyclopedia compiled by Lambert of Saint Omer (ca. 1120), pictures a crowned Antichrist seated upon Leviathan. See Emmerson, *Antichrist in the Middle Ages,* 21, 46, 117, and illus. 1.

360 The devils now begin to dance—probably dancing chaotically or counter-clockwise—to celebrate their initial victory. When Adam and Eve are dragged to Hell in the twelfth-century Anglo-Norman *Play of Adam,* the devils similarly celebrate by making "a great dancing and jubilation over their damnation"; translation by David Bevington, ed., *Medieval Drama,* 105. Although in the *Passion du Palatinus* the devils do not dance, after Jesus is crucified they speak of festivities and merry-making (see ll. 1269–74). For dancing by evil characters in medieval drama see Rastall, "Sounds of Hell," 119–22.

366 The scene shifts back to earth and to Antichrist's Mother, who is now visibly pregnant.

THE GIRL° My sweet and noble lady,
with all my love I implore you not to despair.
Take consolation in yourself
and abandon your sorrow.   375
It will do you no good.
Keep fair hope in your heart,
for Mohammed is so powerful
that he can certainly help you in this affair.

ANTICHRIST'S MOTHER Dear friend, leave off this dispute!   380
You do not feel the ill that I feel.
I am not far from going out of my mind
for having dared to be so brazen
as to sleep with the devil.
It was an astonishingly senseless thing to do,   385
and yet I do not regret it in the slightest
for I am secure in my knowledge that my son is
   destined to be
more powerful than any man yet born or to be born.
That is all that comforts me:
Christianity will expire because of him   390
and the Jews will once again be elevated.

THE GIRL My lady, your belly is fuller
than it was even the day before yesterday.
My suggestion is that we take this path
in order to reach that house over there.   395
It will soon be time for you to lie in;
I am absolutely convinced of it.

ANTICHRIST'S MOTHER My sweet sister, take me there then!
I am very anxious to get there,
for I could really use some rest.   400
Let us be off, my dear friend!°

THE GIRL Lady, your companionship
makes me very happy and full of joy.

---

372 The Girl: MS "La Damoiselle." She plays the role of the midwife, who is included in one group of illustrations portraying the birth of Antichrist. See Blumenfeld-
Kosinski, "Illustration as Commentary," 600–602, figs. 2–6.

401 Antichrist's Mother and the Girl now set off down the path to reach the house
(cf. ll. 394–95), which may be represented by the same bed in which Antichrist was
conceived. They probably reach the house by l. 412. Antichrist's Mother then gets into
bed to deliver her baby, as is shown in min. 12, placed in the MS after l. 417.

I can hardly wait for us to arrive
so that you can receive help and support.   405

ANTICHRIST'S MOTHER My sister, I am no longer able
    to sustain myself,
what a pitiful creature I am!
My sister, take care of me.
I feel terrible pains within my loins.°
Woe is me, what shall I do?   410
I truly believe I will die from this.

THE GIRL Lady, don't be frightened,
for Mohammed will help you
and deliver you very soon.
You are certain to give birth shortly   415
and will then be delivered of your child.
Lady, doubtless you are carrying a handsome son.°

ANTICHRIST'S MOTHER I place all my hope
in Mohammed and his power.
Foolish are all those people, let there be no doubt,   420
who do not admire his miraculous qualities!

AGRAPPART *devil*
My lords, I bring you news:°
Antichrist has been born on earth.
Henceforth we shall be able to overcome
absolutely all the Christians in the world.   425

PLUTO *devil*
May they be destroyed by noxious hellfire!
I cannot contain myself, so truly anxious am I
for them all to be burned in Hell.
Nothing could please me more.

409–11 The painful and despairing pregnancy of Antichrist's mother contrasts with
Mary's joyful pregnancy, often stressed in medieval plays staging the Nativity. Cf.
note to l. 214.

417 In some accounts Antichrist is very handsome and noted for his ability to seduce women. The block-book *vitae Antichristi* in one scene shows him sitting in a
garden with his arm around a young woman. See Boveland, et al., *Der Antichrist*, 4.

422–23 The action now shifts back to Hell, where Agrappart announces the birth to
the assembled devils. The play does not stage or describe the actual birth of Antichrist, which in some accounts is extremely violent; it is sometimes portrayed as a
Caesarian birth, and often the mother dies. See Boveland, et al., *Der Antichrist*, 4; and
Blumenfeld-Kosinksi, "Illustration as Commentary."

SATAN *devil*

    Hazart, I entreat you, may it please you 430
    and Matam, together,
    (for I consider the two of you to be excellent soldiers)
    to go straight to Babylon.
    You will tell the mother of Antichrist
    to teach him our black magic° 435
    and never to remind him of God.
    Go there without any delay!°

HAZART *devil*

    I can hardly believe the day will come
    when I can look at that child.
    I don't wish to sit still any more this morning 440
    until I come to Babylon.

LE MATAM *devil*

    Hazart, my friend, I shall accompany you,
    with the help of Mohammed.
    I do not doubt in the slightest
    that you are very familiar with the route. 445

THE GIRL Lady, look at what a face°
    and what limbs your son has!
    There is no doubt that in the last thousand years°
    no comparable child was born of woman.

HAZART° Lady, I come on behalf of the father 450
    of this child that you are holding here.
    He will be cunning and wise,

---

435 According to Adso, "Antichrist will have magicians, enchanters, diviners, and wizards who at the devil's bidding will rear him and instruct him in every evil, error, and wicked art" (*Libellus*, 91). See Emmerson, *Antichrist in the Middle Ages*, 79.

437 Hazart and Le Matam now set out for Babylon, arriving there and addressing Antichrist's Mother at l. 450.

446–49 The Girl presents Antichrist to his mother. Her description of the baby is deliberately ambiguous, since the tradition sometimes represents him as bestial and demonic, sometimes as handsome and saintly. See McGinn, "Portraying Antichrist."

448 The last thousand years may allude to the orthodox view of the millennium, during which Satan is bound for a thousand years (Apoc. 20:3). Exegetes identified the release of Satan after the millennium with his great increase in power, most evident in the rule of Antichrist. See Augustine, *City of God*, 20.8, p. 911 and 20.19, p. 934; Emmerson, *Antichrist in the Middle Ages*, 79; and Russell, *Lucifer*, 269–70.

450 Hazart and Le Matam enter from Hell. Although only Hazart speaks, min. 15, placed in the MS after his speech, represents both devils dressed in human costume. They stand above the child and the mother, who remains in bed.

so he will need to learn our occult arts.

ANTICHRIST'S MOTHER It is Mohammed I have to thank for this;
I place him under your tutelage.   455

FIRST ANGEL *in song*°
Enoch, Enoch, and you, Elijah,
for the sake of God, leave this place!°
Go and preach to the misbelievers
the law of God that has been established on earth.
Travel forth and go to war,   460
for, to put it bluntly, you will die,
but afterwards you will be resurrected.
I am certain that you are fully aware of this.

ENOCH Tell me, dear friend, have you heard
the command of God?   465

ELIJAH Yes, indeed, fair and gentle companion.
I know perfectly well that the term has arrived,
for an evil man has become
more treacherous than all the devils,
and he will battle us for three and a half years°   470
with an extraordinary hatred.
We must therefore at this juncture
proclaim the faith of Jesus Christ,
announcing and promulgating the good word.
We will have a lot of suffering   475
and we will have to offer up our bodies to death,
but then they will have perfect glory.

ENOCH Dear people, keep in memory°

---

after 455 MS "Premiers anges en chant." The accompanying miniature, placed in
the MS after l. 465, represents an angel emerging from the sky, speaking to Enoch and
Elijah, who stand within a walled garden. The angel's song, ll. 456–63, is set to the
music for *Aeterne Rex Altissime*; see *Jour du Jugement*, ed. Roy, 14; and Appendix 3,
below.

457 The place is the Earthly Paradise.

470–77 Cf. Apoc. 11:3–12. According to most exegetes, Enoch and Elijah preach
against Antichrist for three and one-half years before they are killed by Antichrist or
his henchmen; for the timing of their preaching and Antichrist's rule, see Emmerson,
Antichrist in the Middle Ages, 100–101. The opposition of the Two Witnesses to Antichrist's deceit is the feature most commonly represented in medieval Antichrist drama. The dialogue of Enoch and Elijah here gives them the opportunity to journey
from the Earthly Paradise.

478 Enoch and Elijah now begin to preach against Antichrist. Miniature 17, placed
in the MS after l. 485, shows each standing in a pulpit addressing a large group of

the passion of Jesus Christ,
his death, his resurrection,   480
the way in which he assumed human flesh
in the body of the Virgin, she who is full of all
    the virtues,
and the fact that he is seated at the right hand
of his father, the celestial King.
He is the true God and, just as truly, man.   485

ELIJAH Know you all that at this time
Antichrist has begun to reign,°
he who says that Jesus Christ, the gentle,
was just a man, a faithless enchanter,
and a deceiver of all people.   490
He will forbid belief in Him
and say: "The power is mine
in the sky, on land, and in the seas."
He will then proclaim himself the son of God°
and say that he is the Messiah.   495

ENOCH Pay heed to the prophecies,
believe the law of the Gospels,
so that this demon should not, through his wiles,
have us all condemned
and cast into damnation with the devils.   500
Retain the law of Jesus Christ,
and do not lend any credence to the wonders°
that the aforementioned Antichrist will perform,
for he will act in conjunction with the Devil,
who, with all his legions,   505

---

men and women. In their shared sermon the two prophets review the basics of Christian doctrine. Because Antichrist (cf. ll. 488–90) will deceive the world by preaching
a new doctrine that attacks the divinity of Jesus and that denies that Jesus is the Son
of God (cf. 1 John 4:3), the Two Witnesses oppose Antichrist's false teaching by
concentrating on the incarnation and passion.

487 The sermon of the two prophets serves the thematic purpose of opposing
Antichrist and the dramatic purpose of allowing an unspecified period of time to pass
during which Antichrist matures into a young man ready to begin his rule.

494–95 Enoch and Elijah warn that Antichrist will be the archetypal deceiver,
fulfilling Christ's prophecy: "For many will come in my name saying, I am Christ:
and they will seduce many" (Matt. 24:5).

502–9 In their sermon the Two Witnesses foreshadow the play's action. Antichrist's
apparent ability to perform miracles was much debated and was particularly disturb-
ing to medieval theologians. See Emmerson, *Antichrist in the Middle Ages*, 92–94.

22

will inhabit him.
He will make the dead come to life
and take up residence with the living;
he will make the blind see
and force the most exalted to sit among the abject.   510
It is to the destruction of Christianity
that he will devote all his efforts,
but he does not have the power to do this.

ELIJAH What he is about to do will have the sanction
of God, who will allow all of this to happen°   515
as a consequence of our sins; but once he sees
that Antichrist has accomplished much of what he desired
he will make him suffer in the extreme.
He will cast him down into Hell,
before the eyes of all who are there at that time,   520
both him and his entire clan.

ENOCH Fair lords, I beseech you
to repent, in the name of God.
You can all have my firm promise
that very soon the Antichrist of whom we speak   525
will come here and bring
with him a great multitude.

ELIJAH Be careful not to pay any attention
to him or to those perfidious miracles of his,
for it is a poisonous draught, not a healing elixir,   530
which will completely pollute
all those who place their trust in him.
Instead, protect yourselves often with the
    sign of the cross,
the cross of the benign King,
and with all your devotion pray to God,   535
as well as to his most benevolent virgin mother,
that you will not succumb to temptation.

---

515 Medieval theologians explained that God allows Antichrist to deceive and
persecute the Church in order to test Christians. Augustine notes that those deceived
by Antichrist "deserve to be led astray, 'because,' in the Apostle's words, 'they did
not welcome the love of truth so that they might be saved'" (*City of God*, 20.19, pp.
934–35). On the other hand, Adso warns that "even those who are perfect and God's
chosen ones will doubt whether or not he is the Christ who according to the scriptures will come at the end of the world" (Adso, *Libellus*, 92).

SATAN° I have come to speak to you, fair brother:
　　I am very anxious to bring about your advancement.
　　If you agree to join up with me,　　　　　　　　　　540
　　I shall make you the greatest man
　　who ever was; and believe me,
　　when I have taught you some of my tricks,
　　no man will have a greater reputation than you.
　　You will be lord over the entire world.　　　　　　545

ANTICHRIST By the name of God, in whom all good things abound,
　　I greatly wish to learn about this.

SATAN Then you must listen well to me.
　　You must renounce God
　　and grant everything to me,　　　　　　　　　　550
　　body and soul together.
　　I am the one on whose account the world trembles.
　　I shall cause you to be honored
　　above all others, as well as to be worshiped,
　　provided you give me your promise　　　　　　555
　　that you will never do good, not even once,
　　and instead that you will destroy Holy Church.
　　You will then subjugate
　　the entire Christian world in such a way
　　that all who do not obey you　　　　　　　　　560
　　and continue to speak well of Jesus
　　will be crushed.
　　You will call yourself the son of God.
　　No one will be able to conceal anything
　　without your knowing all about it.　　　　　　565
　　You will be able to distribute gold and other booty.
　　The dead themselves you will bring back to life.
　　Of this you can be sure: You will freely perform
　　your every wish on earth.

ANTICHRIST I want to possess this great treasure.　　570
　　I hereby become your vassal, in body and in soul.°

---

538 The scene now shifts to Antichrist, who has matured into a young man and is
ready to begin his deceitful reign. Although Enoch and Elijah are now offstage, they
continue their preaching (cf. l. 1046) and appear again later to challenge Antichrist
and be killed.

571 Satan's relationship with Antichrist suggests a pact with the Devil, "body and
soul" (cf. l. 551), as well as feudal vassalage. For a popular dramatic version that
presents such a pact in terms of feudal vassalage, see Rutebeuf's *Le Miracle de Théo-*

24

SATAN Then sit down here on this stool.
I wish to bestow my power upon you.
I place in your hands°
all my authority and that of my household,°   575
whose rule extends to every single place.
All that you can possibly imagine
will be accomplished as you wish.
I shall remain with you, never leaving your side;
and I will make all the kings of this domain   580
humble themselves before you.
Be not astonished in the slightest,
for you have the power to do anything to them.
Hurry up and call people to your side;
do your best to show off your might.   585

ANTICHRIST° I have come into the world from my Father,
God the Almighty, the King of glory.
You must, each and every one of you, believe in me,
for I have power over the entire world,
the heavens and the deep sea.   590
I am God the all-powerful,
knowledgeable of all things good and evil.
Now I want you to approach me
and exalt my deeds,
for you have seen me but little on earth,   595
however much you have believed in me.
I can bring anything to pass without exception,
and I have come to this place
in order to lead you to Heaven,

---

phile," 165–92, esp. ll. 239–55.

before 574 A miniature is placed between ll. 573 and 574 and the rubric "SATAM" is then repeated before l. 574.

575 Antichrist receives the authority of Satan, a scene based on Apoc. 13:2, in which the beast from the sea receives the power of the dragon. This is one of the most frequently illustrated scenes in Apocalypse manuscripts.

586 Antichrist begins his reign by preaching to a large crowd. Beginning his parody of the life of Jesus, the first words of his sermon (l. 586) echo those of Christ: "I came forth from the Father, and am come into the world" (John 16:28). In min. 20, placed in the MS after l. 592, Antichrist is dressed as a Franciscan friar, a garb he wears in all remaining miniatures. The association of Antichrist with the Franciscans may reflect the popular antifraternal tradition of the later Middle Ages, which is evident, for example, in the character of Faus Semblant in the *Roman de la Rose*. On its association with the Antichrist tradition, see Emmerson and Herzman, *Apocalyptic Imagination*, 76–103.

whence long ago the angels fell.   600
Should there be one among you who has some illness,
let him come to my side and proclaim it to me,
and I will instantly cure him.
All that I say will be done,
for I can do absolutely anything, let there be no doubt.   605

THE BLIND MAN Dear lord, never once did I see the
    slightest thing,
and I have a great desire to be able to see.
If you heal me
I will believe in you with a loyal heart.

ANTICHRIST Come on over here, you of little faith,°   610
and look at my beautiful deeds!
Mortal, I order you to open
your eyes and see: Look at me!°

THE BLIND MAN Lord, place me under your protection.
If it pleases you, I wish to serve you,   615
that I might thereby merit
your glory, which will never cease.
He who amply serves you will only be the better for it.
I am going to proclaim everywhere, dear lord,
your great power and describe   620
how you gave me back my sight,
which was for all times taken from me.
Never before did I have a greater joy.
Now, fair lords, everyone behold
the great power of this lord.   625
I do not have the slightest doubt
that he is the true Messiah,°

---

610 you of little faith: Antichrist echoes Christ's words in Matt. 6:30, 8:26, 14:31, 16:8, and Luke 12:28.

613 Antichrist's first miracle imitates a similar miracle performed by Christ (Matt. 9:27–30), who, after restoring the sight to two blind men, ordered them not to tell anyone. Like the Blind Man in the play who proclaims Antichrist's power everywhere, however, they "spread [Christ's] fame abroad in all that country" (Matt. 9:31). The Blind Man's witness is later cited by two of the kings (ll. 848–55).

627–29 Jews, not accepting Jesus of Nazareth as the Messiah, await the Messiah promised by the Hebrew prophets. This expectation was one of the beliefs most often attacked in Christian anti-Judaic polemics and one reason why medieval Christians expected the Jews to be particularly susceptible to the wiles of the pseudo-Messiah, Antichrist. Trachtenberg notes that one eleventh-century "formula of renunciation of Judaism requires the convert [to Christianity] to anathematize 'all those who hope for

whom, according to the prophecies,
the good Jews have awaited.

ANNES *a Jew*°
By the law of God, we have heard you well;   630
you have spoken the truth.
Fair lord, if you please,
have people announce publicly throughout this town
your dominion and proclaim that
whoever does not believe in you   635
will be placed along with the wretched
in a dungeon or a prison vault,
and will die there without receiving a sentence.
Make it so that everyone believes in you:
Have coins minted   640
upon which your image is engraved,°
and as soon as they are made
have it announced that everyone should take one
as a sign that they are under your banner.
Let each of them worship your image   645
and should there be found some imbeciles
    (for this would not be wise)
without your ensign,
let them be put to death
as proven traitors would be, without any redemption.

ANTICHRIST You speak well; here is the craftsman   650
who has already made the coins.
Get someone who will cry out loudly enough for all to hear
the instructions you have just devised.

ANNES *a Jew*
Come forth, crier. I have placed in writing

---

the coming of the Messiah, or rather of Antichrist' ''; see *The Devil and the Jews*, 32.

after 629 Annes's name probably alludes to Annas, a Jewish priest who was the
father-in-law of Caiaphas and the first person to whom Jesus was taken upon his
arrest (John 18:13). He often appears in dramatic presentations of the Trial and Crucifixion of Christ, including, for example, *Le mystère de la passion nostre Seigneur*, *Livre
de la Passion*, and *Passion du Palatinus*. Annas is also included among the damned in
Lo Jutgamen General (see *Le Jugement Dernier*, ed. Lazar, 162–63). In our play Annes re-
sponds to the Blind Man (l. 631), who in min. 23, placed in the MS after l. 629, is
shown speaking to a crowd. Beginning l. 632, Annes addresses Antichrist.

641–49 The image on the coins probably alludes to the image and mark of the beast
(Apoc. 13: 14–18). For this scene see Emmerson, *Antichrist in the Middle Ages*, 174–75.

27

the orders of my lord, 655
for he wishes them to be proclaimed
exactly as they are enumerated in the text.
If there is any man who ever places
the coin that you see here
at a greater price than he has ordered, 660
he will have him put into prison.

PLUTO *crier*°

I will handle it smoothly
and do a good job; let no one be afraid of that!
All of you, listen, in the name of the one
who has all four elements° 665
serve him at his beck and call,
he who can make it rain and thunder,
and who can give to everyone
bodily and spiritual health.
Let there not be a single lord, a single woman, 670
who, so confident in his or her power,
would not pay homage to him.
It is he who has had these coins made:
See before you the mold
displaying his countenance. 675
You can be sure, let there be no doubt,
that if anyone shows disrespect or scorn toward it,
he will suffer such great distress
that he will never have a moment's relief.
Take care that whenever it is in your sight 680
you worship it
in all places, and thus pay it tribute.
There is not a baron in the world, of whatever stature,
who would not incur misfortune
were he to disobey or otherwise 685
act against this commandment.

---

after 661 Pluto, the third devil introduced earlier (after l. 227), now plays the role
of a crier. Miniature 25, placed in the MS immediately before his speech, shows Pluto
dressed as a man.

665 The four elements are earth, water, air, and fire. The claim may be based on
Adso's warning that Antichrist "will make fire come down from heaven in a terrifying way, trees suddenly blossom and wither, the sea become stormy and unexpectedly
calm. He will make the elements change into differing forms, divert the order and
flow of bodies of water, disturb the air with winds and all sorts of commotions, and
perform countless other wondrous acts" (*Libellus*, 92).

28

Furthermore, whoever is found or taken into custody
without the ensign will be accused
of disloyalty and put to death.
May no one ever again endeavor   690
to supplicate the son of Mary,
for he would instantly lose his life:
Verily he was a false enchanter,
a traitor, a deceiver,
who never had any regard for the good.   695

THE LEPER For a long time I have been mired
    in pestilence
and still am, which grieves me terribly.
I no longer know where I might go,
lord, nor what counsel I might seek
which could cure me of my illness.   700
I am a leper, and have a putrid body.
I have noticed that even poor beggars
exclude me from their company
because of this disease that they fear
and which is indeed the cause of this
    tremendously foul stench.   705
I beg you, lord, that it please you,
by your most exhaulted power,
to grant me relief from my illness,
which night and day burns me and torments me
and putrefies my miserable flesh.   710
I have put up with so much that I can hardly
    keep from going wild.

ANTICHRIST If I relieve you of your pains,
and you wish to receive a cure,
let me tell you right now
that you must believe in me,   715
for I have power over all creatures
and can perform all things.
You must abandon the disreputable law
handed down by Jesus, the son of Mary.
Then you shall be, have no fear,   720
totally pure, totally fit, totally unimpaired.

THE LEPER Lord, with all my heart I will avidly
    do what you wish.

ANTICHRIST I very much want to cure you,

as well as all those who follow in the tracks   725
of my glory, of my abundant grace.
I wish for your flesh to be completely healed.
With this clear fountain water
wash your hands and your face,
and then you shall pay homage to me,   730
for my powers have healed you.°

THE LEPER You have dried up the pox that lay upon me;
    I know it to be true, I no longer have the slightest trace of it.
    I now place all my hope in you.
    You are the true God, free of dishonor.   735
    To you I give my body and my soul,
    for you are replete with all the virtues.
    We really lived like beasts
    when we used to worship Jesus Christ, the son of Mary.
    May his law be damned!   740
    I no longer care to pray to him.
    Rather do I wish to renounce him in every regard,
    both his law and all his power.

EVIL BISHOP King Antichrist, the proofs you display
    are full of joyous charms,   745
    and your skills are most precious;
    there is no unjustness in you.
    I am the bishop of a city
    whose people are quite astonished
    at what they have seen and heard   750
    and understood to be the truth.
    Those who have delivered themselves to you
    will reside in everlasting joy
    and escape from the hands of the Devil.
    Indeed, you shall lead them to Heaven   755
    and so they desire you. A good ten years°
    ago, or even more, a powerful gentleman,
    who was not miserly toward the poor,
    died; he was truly a sage.
    His death was a terrible pity.   760

---

731 Antichrist's second miracle, curing a leper, again imitates one of Christ's miracles (cf. Matt. 8:2–3). The Leper's witness later influences one of the kings (ll. 862–63).

756 The Evil Bishop now suggests that Antichrist perform his most startling miracle, the resurrection of the dead. The two probably now begin to walk toward the cemetery (l. 761), which they reach by l. 780.

He is resting in this cemetery.
If we could have him come back
to life, just the way he used to be,
then everyone would say
that you are in truth God.   765
They would believe in you unwaveringly
were they to see him resurrected.

ANTICHRIST I am God, full of truth,
  God without end, without beginning,°
  I am God, who neither cheats nor lies;   770
  I am the governor of Heaven,
  leader of all the sainted men and women.
  I do not wish to deceive you;
  I want everyone to know in all its truth
  that whosoever repudiates Jesus Christ,   775
  abjuring both him and his law,
  and applies his thoughts to me,
  will receive the glory of Heaven,
  for I can do all things without any limitation.
  I wish to resuscitate this man   780
  that you brought to my attention today,
  who has lain in the ground for so long.
  You will thus see my manifest powers,
  and judge whether they are not totally evident
  and whether one must not indeed worship me.   785
  Body, pick yourself up instantly!
  I want you to leap out of the earth
  and go to and fro, and walk
  through all places, along all paths,
  strong and handsome, pure, healthy and whole.   790
  Display your body freely.

THE RESURRECTED BODY My lord, you who
  have brought me back to life,°

---

769 Antichrist appropriates the attributes of Melchisedech, which make him like the Son of God (cf. Hebrews 7:3). The speech also recalls the Alpha and Omega of Apoc. 1:8.

792 Antichrist's third and most impressive miracle once again imitates Christ's miracles; cf. Matt. 9:24–26 and, for the resurrection of Lazarus, John 11:43–45. The play here gives no indication that Antichrist's "miracle" is false; it isn't until Beelzebub later leaves the Resurrected Body (after l. 1599) after the destruction of Antichrist that its falsity becomes clear to the audience.

31

it is right for me to do what you will.
You are the true God, full of grace,
replete with kindness and friendship.   795
You have great affection
for all those men and women
who believe in your resplendent powers:
It is in order to protect them from destruction
that you have come to entreat each and every one of them.   800
Those who do your bidding
will all be with you
in Heaven, your abode.

EVIL BISHOP Now I see that, in consonance with reason,
we must put our faith in you.   805
It is precisely in order to wrest us from foolish belief
that you have come among us.
Anyone must be considered foolish
who does not live to serve you:
You have the power of judgment over all things.   810
From now on I will defy Jesus
and remain in your allegiance,
and I will have all my subjects do the same:
It is in you that celestial force is to be found.
I shall tell the people of your powers   815
and will serve you as my God.
I give to you myself and my bishopric.
You have brought back to us the person
that all of us desired
to have once again alive among us,   820
and you have resurrected him.

THE RESURRECTED BODY I am going back within the ramparts°
to see my neighbors from the city.
I am absolutely certain that there are some
ten thousand who will, when they find out   825
about your miracles, have
complete and perfect belief in you.

---

822 The Resurrected Body, now clothed, enters the city, as he is pictured in min. 32,
placed in the MS after l. 813. His witness is the basis for the conversion of the kings
(ll. 834–43).

DAGOBERT *the first king*°

> Lords, speak your thoughts.
> Can this at all be the truth,
> that Antichrist has come to our cities   830
> as the son of God the Father?

MALABRUM *king*°

> Whoever does not believe this will pay for it.
> I can certify that I saw a man
> who had been in the grave ten years:
> I am certain that he resuscitated him.   835

---

after 827 Dagobert is the name of a famous Merovingian king. According to the *Grandes chroniques de France*, the immensely popular vernacular chronicles of the thirteenth and fourteenth centuries, Dagobert founded the Abbey of Saint-Denis. In his political reading of the play Roy unconvincingly identifies the kings with various European nations and Asian peoples; he specifically considers Dagobert to be the King of France (*Jour du Jugement*, 41). It is much more likely, however, that the names reflect literary sources rather than political figures. The author of the *Jour du jugement* demonstrates a broad familiarity with profane fictional works that were popular in the late thirteenth and early fourteenth centuries. In addition to the parallels with the prose *Merlin* the author seems to have been quite a connoisseur of the *chanson de geste* tradition, which was transmitted in huge manuscript cycles throughout this period, some containing as many as a dozen discrete works. The epic tradition represented a popularizing history of France, particularly concentrating on the heroic figures of the Carolingian period, and so would have seemed compatible with the historical and social tapestry depicted in the play. In particular the names of nine of the ten kings occur in one or more *chansons de geste*, and the overwhelming majority of these designate Saracen soldiers or kings. Some, such as Fierabras and Loriquaire (undoubtedly a version of the name Loquifer), are featured in epics of their own (*Fierabras* and *Le Bataille Loquifer*), whereas others, such as Malabrum and Maillefer, are mentioned in a half-dozen different works. The name Dagobert, in addition to belonging to one of the best-known Merovingian kings, was attributed to a Saracen king in several *chansons de geste*, including *Le Couronnement de Louis* and *Le Charroi de Nîmes*. The author was quite taken with the exotic nature of onomastic invention in the epic. Three of the Jews—Malaquim, Corbadas, and Haquim—likewise have names that occur in the epic tradition, all again associated with Saracens, as does the devil Agrappart. Contemporaries probably recognized the play's epic subtext and perhaps delighted in the subordination of such larger-than-life heroic and "historical" figures to God's supernal order. For the appearance of the names in the *chansons de geste* see Moisan, *Répertoire des noms propres*. The number of the kings may also allude to the ten horns of Apoc. 17:12 and Dan. 7:7. According to Jerome's *Commentary on Daniel*, "at the end of the world, when the Roman Empire is to be destroyed, there shall be Ten Kings who will partition the Roman world amongst themselves." The little horn that rises from among the ten horns (Dan 7:8) symbolizes Antichrist, "the man of sin, the son of perdition" (77). Adso simply notes that Antichrist "will first convert kings and princes to his cause, and then through them the rest of the peoples (*Libellus*, 91). See Emmerson, *Antichrist in the Middle Ages*, 44–45.

after 831 Roy finds Malabrum's name the most curious of the Ten Kings; see *Jour du Jugement*, 42–43.

YSOART *king°*
> He is telling the absolute truth.
> The man lives on our street.
> Hardly any time has passed
> since he passed by here just now.

FIERABRAS *king°*
> It is true, I ran into him as he approached;   840
> he was full of praise for Antichrist's deeds
> and was proclaiming to all the people
> "Antichrist is God, have no doubt about it."

ACCOPART *king°*
> Listen, lords, listen,
> everyone today is saying   845
> that Antichrist is in all ways superior
> in his might to God the son of Mary.

ANDOART *king°*
> It is true, I know for certain that he restored
> the vision of a blind man,
> this Antichrist; I can give you his name,   850
> I know for a fact that he was not able to see.

LORIQUAIRE *king°*
> I believe he was the one we saw
> passing by here this morning;
> he was acting very joyfully on account of his sight,
> which Antichrist had given back to him.   855

---

after 835 Ysoart's name resembles that of the Saracen king Ysorez in *Aliscans*, the most popular of the epics in the William of Orange cycle. Interestingly, this epic identifies the Saracens as "la gent a l'Antecris" (the people of the Antichrist).

after 839 Fierabras is a well-known Saracen from the epic tradition who is converted to Christianity; in Huon de Méry's *Tournoiement de l'Antecrist* Bras-de-Fer serves as Antichrist's chamberlain; see Emmerson, *Antichrist in the Middle Ages*, 189–91.

after 843 According to Roy (*Jour du Jugement*, 42) Achoparts or Acoparts were considered barbarous peoples of the East. In the epic *Aliscans* Açoupart is the name of a Saracen clan.

after 847 Roy, arguing that the name Andoart is a variation of Edward, identifies him as the English king (*Jour du Jugement*, 41).

after 851 Roy's political interpretation of the play identifies Loriquaire as the German emperor and notes that a Loricarts is a German mercenary in *Le Mistere du Viel Testament* (*Jour du Jugement*, 41–42). As noted above, the name is probably a variation of Loquifer, a Saracen king in *Le Bataille Loquifer*.

AROFLART *king*°
> Joy has descended to earth
> since he has come among us.
> May there be no one who might refuse
> to go and witness his divine power.

AGOULANT *king*°
> All people bow down to him,   860
> I swear to you by the consecrated flesh.
> I can assure you that he healed
> a vile and ulcerous leper whose stench was abominable.

MAILLEFER *king*°
> He has found a good physician,
> but I cannot have any faith in that   865
> nor do I wish to pay it any heed
> until I have seen his face.

DAGOBERT *king*
> I agree that each of us should do the same;
> it's a good thing to do, it seems to me.
> Let's go to him now, all ten of us together.°   870
> That way we will be more certain of things.

MALABRUM *king*
> By God, it is a great good fortune
> to have the grace of such a lord
> who has no greater above him;
> I give myself to him without reservation.   875

YSOART *king*
> You, lords, I ask you
> how we are to greet him.

---

after 855 Aroflart's name may be a variation on Arofle, another Saracen king in
Aliscans. Roy suggests that Aroflart's name is coined from Rouflart, which is the name
of a devil in the Modane Antichrist and Doomsday play (*Jour du Jugement*, 43).

after 859 Agolant is the name of a Saracen people in *Aliscans*.

after 863 Maillefer, like Fierabras, is a Saracen well-known from the *chansons de
geste*; he is the son of Rainouart, the subject of a group of epics in the William of
Orange cycle.

870 The ten kings have been speaking together in a group, as shown in min. 33,
placed in the MS after l. 831. They now begin to move toward Antichrist, reaching
him by l. 882, when they address him as pictured in min. 34, placed in the MS after
Accopart's greeting.

FIERABRAS *king*

In our greeting to him,
we shall mention the name of Jesus Christ,
for I do not intend to suggest   880
that he is more powerful than Jesus Christ.

ACCOPART *king*

Strong and powerful king, Antichrist,
in the name of Jesus Christ,
    son of God the Father,
who was born of the Virgin mother,
receive our greeting.   885

ANTICHRIST Foolish kings, if you do not change your mind
and have a firm belief in me,
you will suffer a torment
more grievous than any you have ever seen.
I have formed every being;   890
it is I who create and give life to the world,
and who deliver from all their sins
those who choose to live in memory of me.
Accordingly, I will lead them in my glory
to Paradise, of which I am the lord.   895
But Jesus Christ is the most contemptible
man who was ever born of woman,
and so I consider it an especially great dishonor
for you to greet me in his name.

ANDOART *king*

I have heard from many people   900
that you can do all things.

ANTICHRIST Abandon the ignoble law
of Jesus Christ, that scoundrel!
You will then, after your death,
all be partners in Heaven.   905

LORIQUAIRE *king*

I have heard that you will save
those who serve you wholeheartedly.

ANTICHRIST When those who have expressed their will
    to believe in me
depart from this world,
they will go directly to the glory of Heaven   910
that is mine, in body and in soul,

36

and they will be delivered from the flames
of Hell, which is full of darkness.
I will not show any harshness to my people;
on the contrary, they will find me gentle.   915
The people have seen it, I can do anything:
I make the dead come back to life;
I cure leprosy;
I do not allow any to perish
who wish to beseech me with all their heart;   920
I give the blind back their sight.
This is all so well known
that many have accepted it as the truth.

THE RESURRECTED BODY°
    I can certainly tell the truth regarding that.°
    My soul had left my body   925
    and Antichrist gave life back to me:
    Ten years I lay in the earth!

THE BLIND MAN
    Not a single day had I seen the slightest thing
    with these fair eyes of mine.
    I want you to know without any doubt   930
    that, as soon as I heard the stories
    that his powers were so benevolent,
    I prayed to him in good faith,
    hoping that he might wish to provide me a cure
    for the vision that I had lost.   935
    And here he is who gave it back to me
    just as splendid as it seems.

AROFLART *king*
    Your miracles are most evident.
    But one thing astonishes me:
    Namely whether the poor are not hated by you,   940
    inasmuch as you do not give them any of your possessions.

ANTICHRIST I am devoted to all,
    as much to the poor as to the rich,
    as much to the bounteous as to those who produce little,

---

after 923 MS "Corps."
924 Miniature 35, which in the MS follows the speech of the Resurrected Body,
represents him pointing to his empty coffin as proof of Antichrist's miracle.

37

all those who serve me wholeheartedly;   945
they deserve joy in Heaven,
where they will forever be with me.
Those who love me with all their heart
will be partners in my wealth.
Now, so that you may see more clearly   950
that I have all the power in the world,
take a look: Do you see those people who are so threadbare?°
Because of their exceptional poverty, they suffer greatly.
If in good faith they wish to believe in me,
I will give them wealth in abundance.   955

FIRST POOR MAN   Each of us is so exhausted
from hunger that he cannot support himself.
Powerful king, please bring consolation
to these four famished prisoners.

SECOND POOR MAN   Antichrist, you who are called God,   960
hunger is bringing us to a bitter end.
With your generous kindness,
consent to have mercy on us.

THIRD POOR MAN   My heart has become so gloomy from hunger,
lord, that I no longer know what to do,   965
where to go, in order to find
a meal and thereby keep myself alive.

FOURTH POOR MAN   Hey, Death, go ahead and put
      an end to us!
We cannot find anyone who will help us.
Hunger drives us from door to door,   970
and even then we cannot obtain anything.

ANTICHRIST   I will give you an abundance of goods,
provided that you worship me with good intentions
and remain in my faith.
Soon you will enter my fold,   975
and so you must of necessity serve me well
once I have saved you.

FIRST POOR MAN   Never shall I a single day

---

952 Roy misread this line; the MS reads "Veez vous ces genz qui si sont monde."
Antichrist here points to a group of four poverty-stricken men, who now begin to
approach the Kings.

of my life maintain
faith or belief in Jesus Christ:
I renounce him and his image, 980
and place my faith totally in your name.

SECOND POOR MAN King Antichrist, you of great renown,
by virtue of your overwhelming love
please have pity on me.
All of us are at your beck and call. 985

THIRD POOR MAN King, you who exercise justice over all,
in the name of your sovereign power
may you take pity on these prisoners.
We renounce Jesus and his mother.

FOURTH POOR MAN We consider you to be the true Father; 990
you are God and we believe in you.
We all pray to you with our hands clasped together:
Please take pity on us.

ANTICHRIST *to the First Poor Man*
Friend, hold out your right hand to me:
You will take away this suit of clothing 995
and love me with all your heart.
Never again will you be in need.

ANTICHRIST *to the Second Poor Man*
Here now, take hold and accept these goods.
Take it right now, quick, and carry it off,
and console yourself in my name. 1000
From this day forward you will never lack anything.

ANTICHRIST *to the Third Poor Man*
And you, make sure that you at all times devote
your entire being to my service.
In so doing, you can earn such a reward
that you will never be poor. 1005

ANTICHRIST *to the Fourth Poor Man*
Here, good brother, you shall have this gift.
All four of you were really afflicted.
By asking, you have acquired
wealth and everlasting joy.

AGOULANT *ninth king°*
    Each and every person finds you captivating.   1010
    You are God, this I truly believe.
    Lord, please accept me:
    I renounce Jesus and give myself to you.

MAILLEFER *king*
    Each of us likewise is going all out
    to do whatever pleases you.   1015
    May it now be your wish to embrace our souls
    when they take leave of the world.

ANTICHRIST Those who serve me with sincerity
    will not squander any of their efforts:
    This, I bear witness to you, is the truth.   1020
    All without exception will be in Heaven
    by my side, and they will all
    pay me homage, as they will to my Father.
    I am the sun, I am the light,°
    I am joy, I am solace.   1025
    In Heaven, my fortress,
    all my friends will be saved.

DAGOBERT *king*
    Those who love you sincerely
    will be lucky to have been born,
    for they will all be led to Heaven   1030
    in the company of angels.
    Lord, be not a stranger to us,
    for we humble ourselves totally before you.
    Today the word is out everywhere
    that you are God, it is the truth.   1035
    Our bodies, our souls, our citadels,
    all our kingdoms in their entirety
    are under your command.
    We consider you to be the true father:
    We repudiate Jesus and his mother,   1040

---

after 1009 MS "AGOLANT, ix° roy." Roy's edition deletes the numeral.

1024 Once again Antichrist echoes the words of Jesus (cf. John 8:12). The line may also allude to one common interpretation of the mysterious number of the beast, 666 (Apoc. 13:18). Using numerological symbols, exegetes transcribed the number into the Latin "Dic Lux," a reference to Antichrist's claim to be the light. See *Jour du Jugement,* ed. Roy, 37; and Emmerson, *Antichrist in the Middle Ages,* 40–41.

and all of us pay homage to you.

ANTICHRIST Lords, you have done a wise thing.
I forgive you your misdeeds.

VIVANS *a Jew*°
Ah! My heart is pained and full of sorrow.
We must seek some firm guidance,   1045
for two false preachers have come to this land—
two feigned hermits,
two traitors, two hypocrites—
who have forbidden the entire populace
to obey or even attend to   1050
our master regarding any subject whatsoever.

MARQUIM *a Jew*
In the name of the God who brought me into life,
if I can get my hands on them,
I will in the blink of an eye force them to appear
before our master in order to answer for themselves.   1055
May almighty God bring them to ruin,
and shower upon them his anger and his wrath!
How dare they contradict
that all-powerful one!

CORBADAS *Jew*
Marquim, I am well informed: 1060
Look over there at the two fraudulent betrayers
whose words my dear uncle,
lord Vivans, relayed to you.

HAQUIM In the name of my lord, whom the wind,
the sun, and the moon obey,   1065
I swear I am not worth a feather

---

after 1043 The scene now switches to the Jews, who betray Enoch and Elijah. The
names of the Jews are traditional, as is evident in other medieval French drama, such
as *Le mystère de la passion nostre Seigneur*, ed. Runnalls: there, Vivant is head of the
Jews (112), and Marquin (112) and Haquin (142) are opponents of Christ. Here the
Jews first discuss their hostility to the Two Witnesses, point to them (l. 1061), and
then accost them as a group (ll. 1070–81). They are accompanied by two knights, who
take Enoch and Elijah to Antichrist (ll. 1082–91). The four miniatures accompanying
this scene (placed in the MS after ll. 1051, 1063, 1077, and 1085) are more explicit
regarding the sequence of events. Miniature 39 shows Vivans and Marquim telling
Antichrist about the prophets; min. 40 shows them leading the knights to the prophets; min. 41 shows the knights, wielding swords, arresting Enoch and Elijah; and min.
42 shows them delivered to Antichrist.

if I do not manage to get the people of our realm
to make martyrs out of them.
Come along, my dear companions.

MARQUIM You sons of bitches, sinful dogs,　　　　　　　　1070
you filthy traitors and renegades,
disloyal, vile, abject, and foul,
how can the two of you have been so bold
as to abjure, starting last Tuesday,
in this place, as I am told,　　　　　　　　　　　　　　1075
the name of my lord?
You can be sure that you will suffer death for it.

HAQUIM Tomorrow will be a day of misery for you.
Your sermons are ended,
that you can be sure of. You will be soundly beaten　　　1080
and led before our master.

FIRST KNIGHT Take care, hold on tightly to that one,
and make sure he doesn't escape from you.
I will hold this one by his hood
and lead him to my lord.　　　　　　　　　　　　　　1085

SECOND KNIGHT Lord, you must be feeling greater cheer
than you have for some time.
Here we are bringing to you
two deceitful scoundrels who heaped scorn
on your law, and repudiated　　　　　　　　　　　　1090
your power and your name.

ANTICHRIST *to the prophets*
I enjoin you, by the renown
I have both in the heavens and on earth,
to tell me what you have come here
looking for on behalf of the Devil.　　　　　　　　　1095

ENOCH Antichrist, we have white hair
and are miraculously ancient:
Even before the Christians°
we were born of woman here below.
But in the name of God the Father　　　　　　　　　1100
and of the entire Trinity,

1098 Enoch, as a patriarch, and Elijah, as a prophet, symbolize the two "laws"—the
law of nature and the written or Mosaic law—that precede Christianity, the new law
or the law of grace.

without incurring death, we were cast out
of this mortal life;°
He had us abide in the Earthly Paradise
until your coming.   1105

ELIJAH God without end, without beginning,
    sent us to this place
    in order to guide the misguided,
    and to set back on the right paths
    the good people that you are leading astray.   1110
    We are well aware that you can do many things,
    but you will inevitably be thwarted,
    for the devils, through whose agency you perform your deeds,
    will reward you for those deeds in Hell,
    where you will be tortured.   1115
    You will not remain wealthy for very long,
    nor will you enjoy these pleasures on earth,
    for your sins and your immeasurable vices
    will send you tumbling down to Hell.
    They will make of you the most miserable creature   1120
    that was ever brought up on earth.

ANTICHRIST Deceitful hypocrites, putrid churls,
    you are telling lies. I am the son
    of God, who can do anything; and I made
    all things along with Him.   1125

ENOCH Fie! You devious traitor, how dare you
    brag about yourself in this way in front of us?
    You have done so much with your enchantments,
    your ruses, and your lies,
    that you have placed in the devil's power   1130
    nearly the entire human race.

ELIJAH Fie! You bloodthirsty savage beast!
    You are the one that the good prophet David,°
    who was completely enraptured by God,

1103 See note to ll. 151–53.

1133–39 Elijah here identifies Antichrist with Goliath, an Old Testament type of
Antichrist according to Bonaventure: "In the seventh mystery, the anointing of kings,
he [Antichrist] is symbolized by the armed Goliath. For he will be exteriorly magnificent, and he will also speak blasphemies against the people of God." See Bonaventure,
Collations on the Six Days, 15.6, trans. José de Vinck (Paterson, N.J.: St. Anthony Guild
Press, 1970), 219. The iniquitous king (l. 1135) is Saul. See 1 Kings [KJ=1 Sam.] 17:31–
51.

asked the iniquitous king's permission to fight.   1135
    Out of humility he begged God,
    just as though he could see you,
    to order and proclaim
    that you be annihilated.

ENOCH His words have not been forgotten,   1140
    nor have those of the other prophets,
    for they will see very soon the signpost
    of Death, which will appear before you:
    God will avenge all of us on you,
    but first there will occur the events   1145
    that the Scriptures recount.
    Before this happens, you will have us killed;°
    we cannot avoid death.
    But let me assure you, once we have died,
    we will be resurrected.   1150
    Then we will be free of all suffering.

MARQUIM By God the powerful, in this domain
    there is no man so great nor so exalted
    who would speak as those scoundrels
    have just now spoken to our master,   1155
    who is the son of God, the celestial King;
    Let it be to their greatest misfortune!
    Partner, kick that one in the stomach,°
    and I will bash this one's head in.

MALAQUIM They called my lord a beast,   1160
    and said some extremely injurious and
        shameful things to him.
    Don't think for a minute that I will hesitate
    to inflict considerable abuse and humiliation on them.
    Now look, I am exhausted,
    so strenuously have I beaten and pummeled him.   1165

ANTICHRIST My followers, you have had more than enough fun
    beating up those knaves.
    I want to rid them of their misunderstanding.
    They were exceedingly contemptuous toward me,

1147–50 Apoc. 11:7–12.
    1158–65 The two Jews now beat Enoch and Elijah, a scene that is represented in
min. 43, placed in the MS after l. 1159.

but they will no longer have a respite from death.   1170
Grab hold of them and tie them up,
and then kill them without delay.
Be sure that nothing further is said about them.

MALAQUIM We won't carry on a long deliberation over it:
We will lead them directly to their punishment.   1175

ELIJAH Oh, merciful God, you who through your generosity
allowed your blood to flow on the cross,
on which you were hanged for our sake;
you who suffered death and passion,
who at the Ascension went up°   1180
to the heavens, by virtue of your noble power,
and who sit at the benevolent right hand
of your Holy Father, the King of Glory!

ENOCH Sweet God, do not let us slip from your memory!
We commend our souls to you,   1185
and entrust our bodies to the Holy Spirit.
True God, Holy Trinity,
three persons in unity,
one godhead, one essence,
we implore you, by your power,   1190
to save your humble folk.

ELIJAH Fair lords, the time has come
for you to do as you wish.

HAQUIM I would consider myself quite a laggard
if I didn't kill this one with a single blow.   1195

MARQUIM Wait, let me have this blow!
It's over, we are free of them.
They are dead, they cannot possibly be alive,
and yet my whole body is trembling with fear.

HAQUIM By my faith, partner, it seems to me rather   1200
that the earth shook most powerfully.°

1180 Acts 1:9. Elijah's allusion to the Ascension of Jesus here prefigures the raising
into Heaven of Enoch and Elijah later in the play (ll. 1422–29). It may also allude to
the popular expectation that Antichrist will attempt to parody Christ's Ascension by
rising into the sky with the help of devils, whereupon he will be struck down by
Michael or Christ. See Boveland, et al., *Der Antichrist*, 24–25; Emmerson, *Antichrist in
the Middle Ages*, 101–2; and McGinn, *Antichrist*, 129, 132.
1201 An earthquake accompanied the death of Christ on the cross (Matt. 27:51).

45

MARQUIM By my faith, so it seemed to me.
   I am going to ask my lord
   to be so kind as to tell me
   what caused this to happen.   1205
   You who created winter and summer,
   and all other things according to your pleasure,
   By your holy name explain to me
   ‾why the earth quaked just now.

ANTICHRIST You thoughtless fool, that's what
        it seemed like to you: 1210
   It was I of my own volition who caused that to happen.
   Step down from here
   and go get me the Pope,
   that man who snares and then steals away
   my people from me, as I am told.   1215
   He is the one who opposes me
   more than anyone in the world.
   I feel like destroying
   both him and his entire Church.

MARQUIM It will be done according to your wishes.   1220
   I will take my companions along with me
   and you can be sure that I will keep them in line.
   Get up, lords! Let's assemble our troop.°
   Our master has sent us out
   to destroy abbeys and churches,   1225
   along with the clergy, who are of no importance to him.
   Get up, lords! Sound the alarms,
   lest that deceitful Pope manage, through his enchantments,
   to flee from our grasp.

FIRST KNIGHT I have spent a lot of time in countless battalions, 1230
   and know much about war.
   Many a war machine have I seized, many a man
   I have not only captured but killed

Apoc. 11:13 describes "a great earthquake" upon the resurrection of the two prophets.
Antichrist claims that the earthquake is just one of his many wonders (l. 1211).

1223 Marquim now leads the knights as they set out to arrest the Pope and cardinals, whom they bring to Antichrist, the king of l. 1288. This scene is pictured in
three miniatures, which show the knights planning their attack on the Pope (min. 47,
in MS after l. 1229), seizing the Pope (min. 48, in MS after l. 1243), and taking the
Pope and other religious to Antichrist (min. 49, in MS after l. 1257).

during war maneuvers.

SECOND KNIGHT There is not a man on this earth
   I would fear in arm-to-arm combat.   1235
   Many a woman have I made distraught
   and even widowed after meeting her fine husband.

THIRD KNIGHT Pipe down, for we will easily capture
   the Pope and all the cardinals.
   You know that the Emperor°   1240
   is already on our side.

FOURTH KNIGHT We are noble, worthy, and brave.
   Let's go and take him; there he is.

FIRST KNIGHT You go on this side and you go on the other,
   and the rest of you, whatever happens,   1245
   each should hold on to his cardinal
   and make sure he doesn't get away from you.

SECOND KNIGHT May God be merciless to this fraudulent Pope
   and to all his deceitful kind!
   I bring you bad news: 1250
   You have been captured, no defense will help you.
   You must relinquish that faith
   that you have held until today.
   He who created the wind and the rain
   has sent you this mandate through us   1255
   and has also ordered your capture.
   We will lead you to him bound.

THIRD KNIGHT Indeed, we will hold you most securely;
   you cannot extricate yourselves from our grasp.
   Now we will lead them all in order   1260
   before our master, Antichrist.
   Woe be to anyone who wails or cries,
   lest I cut off his head!

FOURTH KNIGHT You must be having quite a celebration,
   you with the red hoods!°   1265
   We are going to turn the skin

1240 In the *Ludus de Antichristo,* reflecting its German perspective, the Emperor is one of the most stalwart opponents of Antichrist; here, although he does not appear on stage, he has joined the ranks of Antichrist.

1265 Red hoods are worn by cardinals.

of each and every one of you just as red—
    you can be sure of it.
You will be killed and cut up into pieces
if you do not forsake that treacherous law of yours,
which defies and contradicts ours.   1270
I advise you to cast it off.

FIRST KNIGHT Now your situation has become totally
    debased, indigent lords;
you have had a large share
in the comforts of this world,   1275
but now you can rest assured,
if you do not quit your foolishness,
that you will suffer great pain and great anguish.
You must forsake your law.

POPE Gentle God, come forth to render your judgment   1280
    and be of succor to us
against these corrupt people
who are laying waste to the Church in this fashion,
by goading and forcing us
to repudiate your most holy name.   1285
I implore you, for the sake of my sheep,°
please do not forget them.

SECOND KNIGHT O king, you whose heart is ennobled
    through power over the lofty and the humble,
and who in all regions exercise   1290
your might and your righteous desires,
do not at present consider us slow,
for we are bringing the apostle to you.°
We also have the cardinals securely in hand:
Here they are right in front of you.   1295

ANTICHRIST My heart is heavy with grief
    when I see the folly of men such as these,
who should get all the people
back on track and put them in touch with the truth.

POPE We believe in the Trinity   1300
    and are indeed true Christians,

1286 The sheep are Christians. The Pope is the head pastor or shepherd of the Church, who follows the injunction of Jesus to Peter, "Feed my sheep" (John 21:17).
1293 The apostle here is the Pope, the spiritual descendant of the apostle Peter.

48

but you are of Egypt,°
an enemy of the human race.
Just this morning I came to the decision
that in the most noble way possible   1305
I would show you your error.
You want to be treated as God:
Bear in mind where you came from,
who you were and what you will become,
as well as how you will endure   1310
the damnation of Hell.
You know very well that steel and iron,
horses, pomp and spectacle,
trumpets and clarions,
power and riches,   1315
houses and fortresses,
none of these appeal to that
sovereign King whose Passion
I read about early this morning.°
But a heart in tribulation,°   1320
pure and expunged of all vice,
this is to him a pleasing sacrifice.
Relinquish every bit of your pride, relinquish it,
and through humility abase yourself.
Fill your heart with sorrow and gloom,   1325
and cry mercy for your misdeeds.
Give up your projects; they are foolish in the extreme.

ANTICHRIST Get yourself over here, false apostle!
  Stop this polemic of yours;
  it can't do you any good.   1330
  Come here and pay homage to me.

FIRST CARDINAL God, how can you countenance this
    presumptuous behavior?
  Why are you allowing this treacherous creature°
  to force your good and loyal Christians
  to renounce you and believe in him?   1335

1302 Egypt, like Babylon, is a biblical symbol of evil. The city where Enoch and
Elijah are killed "is called spiritually, Sodom and Egypt" (Apoc. 11:8).
  1319 The Pope probably refers to a meditation on the Passion read during Matins,
the early morning liturgical service.
  1320–22 Cf. Psalm 50:19.
  1333 MS: "Qui souffrez que cilz desloiaux." We read MS "Qui" as "que."

49

Dear, gentle God, please remember
your loving concern.

SECOND CARDINAL Lord God, we beseech you,
  please grant us wisdom
  so that we might sustain, in honor of you,   1340
  your true faith and belief.

ANTICHRIST False Pope, you must come
  here toward me and worship me;
  You cardinals, no more delay,
  get up and pay me homage   1345
  or your flesh will be torn apart.
  You can be sure (this is no lie)
  that I am God and bear the truth:
  My Father gave me this populace
  to command in its entirety,   1350
  so that I might lead them to Heaven.

POPE *to Antichrist*
  Fie! Satan, you who once were°
  knocked down from the sovereign kingdom,
  it is through your power that this devil, who has
  deceived absolutely everyone, has come to rule.   1355
  How is it that you are welcomed
  by this foolish, disconsolate crowd,
  you who are their mortal enemy
  as well as that of the entire human race?
  Why does God not take away from you   1360
  this power that you hold?
  God, you who sweat blood and tears,
  and who on the cross chose not only to offer up
  your body, but also to endure death for us,
  in order to cast your people out of Hell,   1365
  may it please you to deliver us

1352–55 The Pope here addresses Satan, who, although he has not spoken since l.
585, may have been silently on stage throughout these scenes encouraging Antichrist's
deceit; Satan earlier had promised to be with Antichrist always (l. 579). In art Antichrist is often accompanied by a devil, especially in the block-book *vitae*; see throughout Boveland, et al., *Der Antichrist*, for example. The accompanying miniature (min.
50, placed in the MS after l. 1295), however, does not picture a devil with Antichrist
in this scene. In l. 1353 the Pope also alludes to the Fall of Lucifer (Isaiah 14:12); the
"this devil" of l. 1354 is Antichrist.

50

from this demon's subterfuge.

ANTICHRIST *to the Pope*
    Pope, I can tell that you are getting
    much too heated up, along with these two knaves,
    who will share in your torments.   1370
    I believe you will change your mind.
    Mossé, do you know what I want you to do with them?°
    Place this pope in a truly odious prison cell,
    and as for these other two,
        because of their misunderstanding,
    I will have a word with them.   1375
    I will have you drawn by horses
    if you do not convert to me.
    Take flight from your error, take flight!
    You have remained there much too long.

FIRST CARDINAL Fair lord, I worship you with all my heart,   1380
    and place myself at your disposal.
    I renounce God and holy Church,
    and place my belief in your new law
    at the same time that I reject and repudiate the one
    that we have held for so long.   1385
    I have come to recognize your power
    and I see in you miraculous signs.

SECOND CARDINAL Lord, your indulgence is total,
    this I can tell from looking at your people.
    It neither seems desirable nor appropriate to me,   1390
    inasmuch as my heart is so captivated,
    to remain in Christianity.
    I give myself over to you totally.

ANTICHRIST *to the First Cardinal*
    Dear gentle friend, I in turn give to you
    more land and riches   1395

1372 Mossé probably takes his name from Moses, the great Jewish lawgiver. Antichrist's Jewish supporter in the Chur *Last Judgment* is also named Mosse; see *Churer Weltgerichsspiele,* ed. Schulze, 90–91. Mossé is a Jewish soldier in *Le mystère de la passion nostre Seigneur,* ed. Runnalls, 118. After Antichrist directs Mossé to lead the Pope to prison, leaving the cardinals behind, he turns to his fourth means of consolidating power, persecution and threats of torture (l. 1376). With the Pope absent, both cardinals quickly side with Antichrist. The following lines allude to Antichrist's three other methods of gaining power: false teaching of a "new law" (l. 1382), false miracles and signs (l. 1387), and bribery (ll. 1395–96).

than you could ever have possessed.
All that I have will be yours.

FIRST CARDINAL Fair master, I am staying by your side
and I will obey you;
moreover, I will go among your people   1400
in order to advocate your rule.°

SECOND CARDINAL Fair lord, be advised
that we have come back from every territory.
You are henceforth hated by no one:
Everywhere you are proclaimed lord,   1405
you are treasured and beloved.
No man can betray you.
Do you know why? In truth,
because your powers are all too evident.

FIRST ANGEL *in song*°
You who suffered death   1410
for the sake of Jesus Christ, the son of Mary,
return to life by his will.
You became a martyr for him,
and now you must leave
this vile, corrupt world   1415
in which nothing is pure,
and rise up here to Heaven.

ENOCH God, you whose goodness
no mouth, no tongue, can describe,
we sing your praise, for we have surmounted   1420
the Devil's overwhelming power.

SECOND ANGEL Enter that perpetual joy
which will never come to an end.

THE GOOD CHRISTIAN° Oh, dear God, you are the one

1401 After this speech the two cardinals set out, moving on stage among Antichrist's followers before returning and addressing Antichrist again beginning l. 1402.

after 1409 MS "Anges premiers en chant." The angel's song (ll. 1410–17) is again set to music, this time for *Veni Creator Spiritus*. See *Jour du Jugement*, ed. Roy, 15 (which misnumbers these lines as ll. 1510–17), and Appendix 3, below.

1424 The Good Christian: MS "Li bons crestiens." This character represents the entire class of those who remain faithful to Christ; the lines are spoken by one actor, who speaks in the singular ("I saw with my own eyes," l. 1425), while referring to the faithful in the plural (l. 1424). Miniature 55, placed in the MS before l. 1442, pictures Mossé attacking one Good Christian; they are watched by a large crowd, perhaps

who will help us,
you who, as I saw with my own eyes,   1425
made it so that those men who for three days°
lay dead in the middle of the city°
have been resurrected to life
and carried off to Heaven!
Each and every one of you, be consoled   1430
that whoever places his faith in God,
and, instead of idolizing Antichrist,
worships holy Church,
will as a recompense have his soul ensconced
in everlasting joy.   1435

MOSSÉ Over here, scoundrel, your deceitful hypocrisy
   will not do you any good,
   and this in spite of the son of Mary,
   whom you have just recalled:
   You would have been better off keeping quiet.   1440
   Never again will you say such things,
   that's how you will be handled.
   All those who witness this
   will circulate the news among the people:
   May the Devil carry them off to Hell!   1445

MALAQUIM I bring you dreadful news.°
   I am being eaten up with great pain and fury,
   because those men you had killed the other day
   have come back from the dead.
   This is an event that you cannot keep   1450
   from being known throughout the city.°
   I can assure you that there are now a good two thousand

---

representing those evil persons who witnessed in fear (Apoc. 11:11) the resurrection
of the two prophets.

1426 Cf. Apoc. 11:11: "And after three days and a half, the spirit of life from God
entered into them."

1427 Cf. Apoc. 11:8.

1446 The scene shifts from the Two Witnesses and the attack on the Good Christian
back to Antichrist, whom Malaquim here addresses. Malaquim's name is traditional;
see *Le mystère de la passion nostre Seigneur*, ed. Runnalls, 200. The name may refer to
Malchus, the servant of the high priest whose ear was cut off by Peter during the
arrest of Jesus (John 18:10).

1451 Malaquim's concern to keep the resurrection of Enoch and Elijah quiet recalls
the attempt by the Jewish priests to silence the guards after the Resurrection of Jesus
(Matt. 28:11–15).

who know about it, and who, having rejected
your law, believe in Jesus Christ.
This is turning into a great disaster for you.   1455

ANTICHRIST All those people are foolish and lacking any sense°
who believe this to be the truth.
They have not been resurrected,
nor have they come back to life.
You can be sure that this is not said out of envy.   1460
According to my plan, I made it so that
they seemed to be alive once again,
all in order to deceive the Christians.
In this way we could maintain our surveillance
and see if we might not hear   1465
someone rejoicing over it
and saying that the son of Mary
had brought them back to life.
But I swear to you with my solemn oath
that if anyone ever puts his faith in him,   1470
he will die for it, no matter what.

SAINT JOHN THE EVANGELIST° Come, brothers, let me give to you,
on behalf of him who lives and rules
over all kings and all domains without exception,
these vials; take one here   1475
and hold it in your hands,
up until the moment you are told
where each of you will go
to pour out the contents of his vial.
Do it in accordance with the message   1480
you have already heard regarding this.
Almighty God, who does not forget
his friends' declarations,
placed by virtue of his command

1456–71 Antichrist now claims to have resurrected Enoch and Elijah himself as a
trap to discover any remaining Christians. He thus claims the miraculous act of God
as his own. His last words are, ironically, a threat (l. 1471).

1472 John is symbolized by the eagle, one of the four living creatures that surround
the throne of God in Apoc. 4:7–8. For the medieval understanding of his life, see
Jacobus de Voragine, *Golden Legend*, 1:50–55. John now distributes to the angels, the
"brothers" of l. 1472, the vials (l. 1475) of wrath, taking the role played by "one of the
four living creatures" who, in Apoc. 15:7, "gave to the seven angels seven golden
vials, full of the wrath of God." This scene serves as a dramatic transition from the
life of Antichrist to the events of the last days that lead to the Last Judgment.

the wrath of his indignation 1485
in the vials: He intends
to avenge the human race
against that filthy and ruthless Beast
who has held sway for so long as God.
Do you see the glorious Temple° 1490
which is already totally filled with smoke?
The entry will remain closed to absolutely everyone
until you have accomplished
the deed that you have begun,
for thus has God ordered it. 1495

THIRD ANGEL Let us all praise the crowned King,°
the Son of God, who thus commands
his saints, and grants them victory
over all tribulation.

FOURTH ANGEL We fervently pray to you on behalf of
your people, 1500
King of kings and Lord of lords:°
May your empire forever be praised,
along with your very holy majesty!

GOD° Work quickly and ready yourselves:
Go and spread my wrath over the earth. 1505
Neither lock nor key will be able
to provide a refuge from me.
Go quickly, for I could not a second longer
endure the great sins
with which the world is stained. 1510
The moment of truth has come for those evildoers.

1490–95 Cf. Apoc. 15:8.
1496–1503 The praise of God echoes the praise of the angels in Apoc. 16:5–7.
1501 Cf. Apoc. 19:16.
1504 In this play, as in the Provençal *Jutgamen General* (see *Le Jugement Dernier*) and
the doomsday plays of the English cycles, the figure of God combines attributes of
both God the Father and the Son, a notion based on the words of Jesus (cf. John
14:10). Usually Jesus Christ, upon his Second Coming, is the judge, a role conferred
upon him by God the Father (cf. John 5:22).

FIRST ANGEL *with vial*
Without a moment's delay I will pour
mine out over the ignoble tribe,
full of great disloyalty,
those who worshiped the filthy beast.°   1515
They are all brimming with cruelty:
In the name of God, I condemn them.

VIVANS Ah! By God's law, my lord Annes,°
I can easily see that we are all done for.
My heart is totally confounded,   1520
for I see that our people are already dead.

SECOND ANGEL *with vial*
I bring you bad tidings,
you who killed the saints.°
Your power has become too strong:
I shall empty my vial over you   1525
and instantly give you back
the recompense for your misdeeds.

CORBADAS God, you gave us the gift
of being born on earth of woman:
Now, as we die such a bitter death,   1530
we curse you with all our power.°
All of us in unison say,
"Cursed be your great power!"

THIRD ANGEL I shall cast God's sentence
upon you who composed   1535
obscure scriptures concerning Jesus Christ,
you who with your false slanders
have sent more than a thousand souls to Hell.
Your rivers and your fountains°

1515 Cf. Apoc. 16:2.

1518–21 Vivans, who had led the opposition to Enoch and Elijah (cf. ll. 1044–51),
addresses Annes, the leader of Antichrist's Jewish supporters, the "our people" of l.
1521. Unlike the *Ludus de Antichristo,* which stages the conversion of the Jews to
Christianity by Enoch and Elijah, this play emphasizes the destruction of the Jews
through the speeches of Vivans, Corbadas (ll. 1528–33), Annes (ll. 1570–79), and
Caiaphas (ll. 1592–99). *Lo Jutgamen general* (see *Le Jugement Dernier*) is similarly unfor-
giving of the Jews.

1523 Cf. Apoc. 16:6.

1531–33 Cf. Apoc. 16:11.

1539–40 Cf. Apoc. 16:4.

will all be completely filled with blood. 1540
These are the wages you have earned
for the blood you spilled
and caused to be spilled through your false words.

FOURTH ANGEL God is just and irreproachable,
without end and without beginning. 1545
He it is who rendered so true a verdict
against those who martyred
these prophets: Each and every one
harvests according to his misdeeds.

SEVENTH ANGEL° God, you who do wrong to no creature, 1550
your deeds are just and true:
Take good care of your saints' wounds.
Your honest verdicts are just°
and you render judgment over all equitably.
Peace, honor, and joy be yours! 1555

FOURTH ANGEL *with vial*
As for me, I will pour out mine
over Antichrist, who proclaimed himself°
to be the Son of God, and who thus ridiculed
the true God of all creation.
His fate will indeed be horrible, 1560
and issue from the sun itself, which will°
become so blazing that he will be snuffed out
by the uncontrollable heat.
Those people that attended to him

1550 MS "vii^e anges." Roy mistakenly reads as "vi^e anges."

1553–54 Cf. Apoc. 16:7.

1557 Antichrist is now destroyed and silenced forever. This scene is unusual, since according to the tradition, Antichrist is killed "by the spirit of [Christ's] mouth" (2 Thess. 2:8). Exegetes disagreed on the manner of Antichrist's death, expecting that he would be killed either by Christ at his Second Coming or by Michael. The archangel kills Antichrist at the end of the Chester *Coming of Antichrist*; see Emmerson, "'Nowe Ys Common This Daye,'" 106–15. In the Modane *Mystère de l'Antéchrist* Michael kills Antichrist when he attempts to parody Christ's Ascension; see *Mystère de l'Antéchrist*, ed. Gros, 16; and Meredith and Tailby, eds., *Staging of Religious Drama*, 106. In the Perugia *Last Judgment* (see *Perugia Last Judgment Play*, ed. de Bartholomaeis, 38) he is killed by Gabriel, whereas he is not killed on stage in the *Ludus de Antichristo*, but flees when "there is a crash of thunder over [his] head" (trans. Wright, 98). On the death of Antichrist, see Emmerson, *Antichrist in the Middle Ages*, 101–03, 141–44.

1561–63 In the biblical account the Fourth Angel pours a vial of wrath upon the sun, "and it was given unto him to afflict men with heat and fire" (Apoc. 16:8). The play conflates this punishment with the blazing destruction of Antichrist.

will experience such an incredible conflagration 1565
that no force, no perseverance
will prevent them from perishing in the heat:
For they obey Antichrist
and believed in his feats.

ANNES I can see that we have been betrayed. 1570
I don't even have the time to repent,
for that God who tells no lies
has already sentenced us.
Cursed be his great power,
his great renown, his great force, 1575
cursed be winter and summer,
and the overwhelming might of God!
I am the most miserable of all;
my tongue is already shriveled and charred.

FIFTH ANGEL *with vial*
My vial will be emptied out 1580
over the wicked beast's throne°
as well as over the entire despicable tribe.
They will soon be cast down to Hell.
I can already see them receive their recompense
for the harm they did to holy Church, 1585
in that place where all will come to judgment,
in Hell, which is so very putrid.
Deceitful traitors, foul villains,
you who voice your incantations
against the Ten Commandments: 1590
Those commandments will never again be desecrated by you.

CAIAPHAS° Our days of high living are over.
May he who created everything be damned!
I can see now the terrible power of those Ten
Commandments that we violated: 1595
We will forever more burn
in Hell, with no possibility of redemption.

1581 Cf. Apoc. 16:10.

1592 Caiaphas: MS "Caiffas." Another Jew, who speaks here for the first time; he
takes his name from the high priest who conspired against (Matt. 26:3) and tried Jesus
(Matt. 26:57). Caïphes appears with Annes in *Le mystère de la passion nostre Seigneur*,
ed. Runnalls, 114; and Cayfas is among the damned in *Lo Jutgamen General* (see *Le
Jugement Dernier*, ed. Lazar, 160–61). It is ironic that Caiaphas is here punished for
violating the Ten Commandments (ll. 1590–91, 1594–95), the heart of the Mosaic Law.

This everyone must believe and know,
that we necessarily will come to such an end.

BEELZEBUB *speaks in the Resurrected Body*°
I have brought this body to its feet   1600
and yet it is lacking the breath of life:
Whatever words he has spoken
are of my doing, for thus I have guided him.
I hereby relinquish him, and head for the agony
of Hell, where I make my abode.   1605

SIXTH ANGEL *with vial*
I wish to accomplish God's miracles
with respect to those powerful men who, arrogant and evil,
have been miserly toward the poor.
Neither their might nor their wealth,
neither their nobility nor their fame,   1610
none of these will help them, this is beyond doubt.
I want to empty my entire vial on them.
There, it has been broken over them.
That great river has withdrawn,°
and you can be sure, with no one left to rescue,   1615
that it will once again be possible to pass safely,
and without getting the slightest bit wet,
over the great body of water that used to flow there.
It's done, there's nothing left.
Now the evildoers can easily see   1620
that Antichrist has deceived them.

THE BLIND MAN Gentle God, my heart has been inspired°

---

after 1599 MS "Baucibuz parle au corps resuscité." The true nature of Antichrist's most impressive "miracle" is finally revealed. The accompanying miniature shows Beelzebub, now a grisly demon, walking away from a supine body, while a nearby crowd gestures in amazement.

1614 The great river is the Euphrates, over which the Sixth Angel pours out its vial in Apoc. 16:12. The river has not been mentioned before in the play, and it is not pictured in the accompanying miniature, which shows an angel pouring out its vial onto a group of people. In the play the river may symbolize the deceit of Antichrist, which is now "dried up" with his destruction.

1622–39 The Blind Man now repents. Along with the Leper and the kings (ll. 1670–87), he represents the third response to the events concluding Antichrist's career: The reconversion to Christianity. The Good Christians symbolize those few who remained faithful throughout, and the Jews those who do not repent and are therefore damned. The tradition expected a brief period of forty or forty-five days to pass after Antichrist's death to allow those deceived, as Adso states, "to do penance because they were led astray by the Antichrist" (*Libellus*, 96). On events after the death of Anti-

to serve you. Repent
I must, for having dared to consent
to repudiate your person   1625
and at the same time worship the creature
who only hinders good Christians.
Jesus Christ, mighty King without bound,
I was crazy when I dared to disavow
you, and directed my prayers to Antichrist,   1630
just because he gave me back
my sight, which I have once again lost:°
I know it is true, I can see nothing.
Merciful God, foolish is he who does not fear you.
Lord, I have done you a terrible wrong   1635
because of a sin that had inflamed me:
It was a crime of folly that I committed against you.
I ask for your mercy, dear God;
may you be compassionate toward me.

LE MATAM° I have every reason to hate the heavenly God: 1640
We shall all be in despair because of him.
We are bereft of our lavish arrogance
and this will be our torture.

SATAN I say to you, my only desire is
to initiate a great war against the one   1645
who formed heaven and earth,
such is the misery into which he has placed us.
Let's go enlist our friends,
for I suggest, whatever happens,
that we do battle with him.   1650

---

christ, see Emmerson, *Antichrist in the Middle Ages,* 101–7; and Robert E. Lerner, "The Refreshment of the Saints: The Time After Antichrist as a Station for Earthly Progress in Medieval Thought," *Traditio* 32 (1976): 97–144.

1632–33 The Blind Man loses his sight, once again proving the falsity of Antichrist's marvelous powers.

1640 Following the pouring out of the vial by the Sixth Angel, Satan and the other devils make plans for a great battle against God (cf. Apoc. 16:14). This is the play's version of the battle of Armageddon (Apoc. 16:16), which ends with the figures of evil "cast alive into the pool of fire, burning with brimstone" (Apoc. 19:20). The importance of this scene is evident in the two miniatures that dominate the top of MS fol. 26ᵛ. Miniature 69, placed before l. 1644, shows four devils in a war council; min. 70, placed before l. 1660, pictures the arming of the devils. Although the play as extant does not stage the battle, it may have been part of the original text lost in the lacuna following l. 1675.

I hate him so much that I cannot be his friend.

LE MATAM These words are not to be scorned:
Indeed, we would do well to keep them in mind.
Beelzebub, you must
come along and fight with us.   1655
You are very good at diving into the thick of it
and accomplishing most
of what you desire.
Let's join with Satan.

BEELZEBUB My feet will not come to a halt   1660
until I have assembled for you
the troops of twenty-five nations,
including giants and pagan gods,°
to combat the Christians.
There is nothing I hate more.   1665
Let us leave directly and in utmost haste,
I am afraid that he will wreak vengeance upon us,
that evil Judge who has so vilified
those who gave themselves over to us.

THE LEPER I can easily see that God has sent   1670
miracles down to earth today.
With all my heart I want to go before him and appeal
my misdeed, may he have mercy on me!
God, you who are filled with almighty power,
Jesus Christ, Son of God the living Father.°   1675

1663 including giants and pagan gods: MS "de jayans et de Jupïans." The meaning
of the line is unclear, but Beelzebub may allude to the expectation that Satan, after
being chained in Hell for a thousand years, will be released "and seduce the nations,
which are over the four quarters of the earth, Gog and Magog, and shall gather them
together to battle" (Apoc. 20:7). In some accounts Gog and Magog are giants, whereas
in other accounts they are specific nations, usually, as in the *Pseudo-Methodius*, twenty-
two nations, which may be a version of the twenty-five nations Beelzebub mentions
in l. 1662. In the Modane Antichrist play they are kings who appear during the first
day of the performance, bringing their armies to support Antichrist; see *Mystère de
l'Antéchrist*, ed. Gros, 62–84. On Gog and Magog see Andrew Runni Anderson,
Alexander's Gate, Gog and Magog, and the Inclosed Nations (Cambridge, Mass.: Mediaeval
Academy of America, 1932); and Emmerson, *Antichrist in the Middle Ages*, 84–88. The
term "Jupïans," which we translate "pagan gods," may echo Adso, who notes that
Antichrist will raise himself in pride over "all the heathen gods, Hercules, Apollo,
Jupiter and Mercury, whom the pagans think are gods" (*Libellus*, 94).

after 1675 A folio is lost here. The missing passage may have staged the play's
version of Armageddon (see note to ll. 1640–69); it probably also included speaking
parts for the first seven kings, since Aroflart, the eighth king, is the next to speak

AROFLART *eighth king*
> I don't wish to delay any more:
> I pray to Jesus with my whole heart
> that he place me back on the path
> by which I will be able to obtain his love.

ANDOART *ninth king*
> Nothing is worth as much as that gift, 1680
> namely the love of God the Father.
> I wish wholeheartedly to entreat his mother,
> that she may bring me into harmony with her son.

MAILLEFER *tenth king*
> Before sin embraces us any more,
> let us pray to holy Mary the beautiful, 1685
> Mother of God, the Virgin maid,
> that she may make our peace with God.

> ### All together°

> Virgin, our Lady full of grace,°
> we feel that we have sinned against God
> and we repent with a sincere heart 1690
> and out of true contrition.

GOD *Finis sum* and the beginning,°
> I shall be without end, and I rule without end.
> My kingdom is without a beginning,
> I am God over all nature, 1695
> I have created every creature
> and ordered all time.

---

when the action resumes.

after 1687 MS "Rerum simul." Presumably these lines would be spoken by all ten kings introduced earlier (ll. 828–67).

1688 Although the Virgin Mary has not been introduced, she must now appear on stage, since here she is addressed in person. The miniature accompanying this scene, placed in the MS before l. 1692, pictures the ten kings kneeling before her, while Christ is enthroned next to her in a Gothic arch. The kings's entreaty begins one of the most solemn, lengthy, and ritualized actions in the play. Various groups (kings, angels, saints) are introduced in order, speak, and then move toward Mary to ask for her intercession while Christ seated in Judgment watches silently.

1692 *Finis sum:* I am the end. The action now turns to the Last Judgment as Christ speaks this line echoing the traditional beginning of Last Judgment plays: "I am Alpha and Omega; the beginning and the end" (Apoc. 21:6; cf. Apoc. 1:8, 22:13).

So much have the people of the world°
surrendered themselves to sin in these times
that there is nothing left that is pure, inviolate, clean: 1700
All have offered themselves to sin.
Too long have I put up with their wickedness;
in truth I will stand for it no longer,
for they are without repentance.
I am just; it is right for me to judge   1705
in the manner of a true judge.
I wish to resurrect all the dead,°
absolving the good of every evil,
and relegating the wicked to the filth
of Hell; all those still to be found in the world   1710
will die in a conflagration.
Then those who have proven themselves will be
in paradise, in body and soul,
and the wicked will forever reside in flames,
without finding any consolation.   1715

CHERUBIM° The All Powerful intends to realize
a plan that he has devised:
He says that he wants to see ended
the existence of the human race,
without leaving the slightest remnant,   1720
and then he will rejoin body and soul.
Let us now go and pray to the Lady°
who is both mother and daughter to him,
that she might pray both to her Son and her Father
for the sake of her people.   1725

SERAPHIM° That is good advice.

1698–1701 The description of the evil of the last days recalls the evil in the days of
Noah (cf. ll. 44–53), when God decided to destroy the world with a flood (Gen. 6:5–7).
Jesus made the comparison between the two periods and their destructions in Matt.
24:37–39.

1707 Cf. Apoc. 20:13.

1716 The Cherubim and Seraphim, who speak next, are groups of angels who are
part of the nine-fold angelic hierarchy. They are probably each represented by one
actor, and are distinguished from the angels who poured out the vials of wrath onto
Antichrist's followers. The Cherubim may appear with four faces and four wings (cf.
Ezek. 10:21).

1722 Up to this point the Cherubim has been speaking to the Seraphim. They now
move toward the Virgin Mary, whom they address beginning l. 1729.

after 1725 The Seraphim may appear with six wings (cf. Isa. 6:2).

Let us go and make our entreaty,
which is most just and honorable.
My Lady, you who are the wellspring
of grace, and light of the heavens,° 1730
pray to your Son in behalf of the world,
dear Lady! that he not topple it
into Hell, that most terrible abode.

CHERUBIM Lady, wise and valiant queen,°
you who illuminate all of Heaven, 1735
Queen above all other queens,
supplicate your Son for the sake of your people.

SAINT JOHN° My Lady, from whom all joy emanates,
on earth as well as in the heavens,
I ask of you a boon 1740
and beseech you—for I have great fear—
in remembrance of how I worshiped
your dear Son when still in my mother's womb:°
Please entreat both your Son and your Father
to have mercy on his people. 1745
My heart is blackened with fear.
Alas! I dare not speak to him,
my Lady: Beg him to remember us
as well as his friends,
dear Lady, for it is not fitting 1750
that we leave your company

1730 Medieval hymns often praise Mary in language associating her with light, illumination, and dawn; cf. l. 1735.

1734–36 In medieval belief Mary is Queen of Heaven as well as Mother of God. In the twelfth century the Coronation of the Virgin by Jesus became a popular subject of medieval art.

1738 John the Baptist (cf. l. 1754), rather than John the Evangelist. On stage he is probably costumed in a rough shaggy fur or perhaps, as John in the *Baptism and Temptation of Christ*, he is shown "with a long beard and with a robe made of camel's hair" (ed. Elliott and Runnalls, 55). He may also hold his attribute, the *Agnus Dei* (Lamb of God; cf. John 1:36). See Jacobus de Voragine, *Golden Legend*, 1:328–36. He now introduces speeches by a series of saints associated with the life of Jesus, all of whom were martyred for their beliefs and preaching. A similar group of saints is included in the *Berliner Weltgerichtsspiel* and the Modane *Jugement de Dieu*; see *Le Jugement Dernier*, ed. Lazar, 26.

1743 John the Baptist was the son of Mary's cousin Elizabeth (Luke 1:36); when Mary and Elizabeth met, John, recognizing the unborn Jesus as Lord, leaped for joy in Elizabeth's womb (Luke 1:41–44). In art John is often portrayed as a child worshiping Jesus and Mary.

and descend with the wicked.
I have placed all my hope in you:
You are well aware that I baptized him°
and preached his coming.   1755
For his sake I lived most abjectly
and even was beheaded for him.°
Sweet Lady, if you wish
you can certainly protect each and every one of us.

SAINT PETER° My Lady, may it please you to listen to   1760
my prayer, which I wish to present to you.
Beg your noble Son
to have it in his heart to contain his anger
and to allow those who served him on earth
to remain in his service.   1765

SAINT PAUL° I as well, Lady, wish to request
your good offices in imploring
your Son to grant
pardon to those who cherished him
on earth, and called him their Lord.   1770
You can be sure that I am terribly afraid.

SAINT PHILIP° Very dear Lady, whom I adore,
and who is venerated in the heavens,
worshiped above all women,
reconcile your Son with your followers,   1775
and beg him to please
have mercy on his people.
My heart is blackened with fear;
I am trembling all over and don't know what to do.

SAINT ANDREW° My Lady, full of grace,   1780

1754–55 Cf. Matt. 3:13–17.

1757 Cf. Matt. 14:3–12.

1760 St. Peter is the leader of the apostles and, according to tradition, the first Bishop of Rome. On stage he may hold his attribute, a set of keys, which represents the Church's control over the gates of Heaven (cf. Matt. 16:18–19). See Jacobus de Voragine, *Golden Legend*, 1:340–50.

1766 St. Paul, probably the most influential theologian and missionary of the Early Church, may hold his attribute, a sword, the means by which he was beheaded. See Jacobus de Voragine, *Golden Legend*, 1:350–64. Miniature 74, placed in the MS after l. 1771, pictures him and other saints kneeling before the Virgin Mary.

1772 St. Philip, another apostle, may hold his attribute, a cross, symbolizing his martyrdom in Scythia. See Jacobus de Voragine, *Golden Legend*, 1:267–68.

1780 St. Andrew, the brother of Peter (John 1:40) and one of Christ's earliest disci-

queen of mercy,
make peace between your people and your Son,
and with utmost gentleness beg him
to bestow his grace
upon those who have served him with a loyal heart,   1785
lest those avaricious ones who were so disloyal
become masters and lords over them.
I tell you, I have greater fear
than I ever did a single day of my life.

SAINT BARTHOLOMEW° Sweet Lady, Virgin Mary,   1790
   you who are queen of the archangels,
   would that I could recall to you
   that greeting that the angel proffered you°
   when you conceived without sin,
   in order that you might hear my prayer   1795
   and beseech God,
   who was incarnated within your loins
   and who delivered us from death,
   to rescue, if he will, his people
   from Hell, and count them among the saints.   1800
   I am afraid; I dare not look at him.

SAINT JAMES° O Queen in whom is enclosed
   all bounty, all beauty,
   all faith, all honor,
   my Lady, dispenser of grace,   1805
   direct a prayer to your beloved Son
   for the sake of your friends, that he not condemn,
   that he not damn them with the wicked.
   I am more frightened than I can say.

SAINT BARNABAS° We have all come to death and martyrdom.   1810

---

ples, may hold his attribute, an X-shaped cross, symbolizing his martyrdom in Greece. See Jacobus de Voragine, *Golden Legend*, 1:13–21.

1790 St. Bartholomew, another apostle and a missionary to India, may hold his attribute, a large knife and possibly a human skin, representing his death by being flayed alive. See Jacobus de Voragine, *Golden Legend*, 2:109–16.

1793–94 Cf. Luke 1:28.

1802 St. James, brother of John the Evangelist (Matt. 4:21) and missionary to Spain, may hold his attribute, a pilgrim's staff or a scallop shell, symbolizing his pilgrimage to Spain and his association with the shrine at Santiago de Compostella. See Jacobus de Voragine, *Golden Legend*, 2:3–10.

1810 St. Barnabas, one of the first Christian missionaries and a companion of Paul,

Most beloved Lady, fountain of compassion,
do not spurn my sobbing and my weeping:
May it not displease you to hear my prayer!
Do not scorn my weeping and my sobbing.
In the name of your holy Son and his passion,   1815
Listen gently to my entreaty, Lady,
I am so afraid, I cannot tell you.

SAINT SIMON° Very dear Lady, soften the anger
of your Son which has become so intense:
May it not be turned toward us   1820
nor toward the others who serve him.
I am afraid of those traitors°
that I see over there: So much do I
    fear their influence—
may he not cast us away from him!—
that I dare not look upon him.   1825

JUDAS MACCABAEUS° Well protected is he who
    has you as his guardian.
May you, dear Lady, gaze upon me with pity
and place us under your care,
along with all those who have cherished you.

---

may hold his attribute, a flame, symbolizing his death by fire. See Jacobus de Voragine, *Golden Legend*, 1:318–21.

1818 St. Simon, known as Simon Zelotes (Luke 6:15), was another apostle who became a missionary to Egypt and Syria. He may hold his attribute, a gibbet in the shape of a cross, representing his martyrdom. See Jacobus de Voragine, *Golden Legend*, 2:260–65.

1822–23 It is unclear to whom Simon refers as traitors; perhaps the devils are already waiting on one side of the stage to carry the damned to Hell (cf. ll. 2076–95, 2382–2407), as often happens in Last Judgment plays.

1826 MS "Judas Cabeus." Judas Maccabaeus, the military leader of the Jewish revolt against Antiochus Epiphanes (1 Maccabees 1–6) around 160 BC, is the only pre-Christian speaker in this sequence. Placed in Heaven by Dante (cf. *Paradiso*, 18:40), Judas Maccabaeus is perhaps included in the play because he opposed Antiochus Epiphanes, an Old Testament type of Antichrist. See Adso, *Libellus*, 90; Emmerson, *Antichrist in the Middle Ages*, 44–45; and McGinn, *Antichrist*, 26–27. In medieval legend Judas Maccabaeus is one of the Nine Worthies or military heroes: three are Jewish (Joshua, David, Judas Maccabaeus), three pagan (Hector, Alexander, Julius Caesar), and three Christian (Arthur, Charlemagne, Godfrey of Bouillon). Although it is possible that other worthies appeared in the play and that their speeches have been lost with the missing folio following l. 1829, no others are listed in the dramatis personae (fol. 1ʳ–1ᵛ).

. . . .

[MOTHER OF GOD]° Son, for whom I was in
    sorrow and pain,   1830
    that day I saw you die on the cross,
    fair Son, may you remember me:
    I entrust myself completely to you.
    Fair, gentle Son, I ask nothing of you
    that would be against your will: 1835
    I beg you to allow those who have venerated me
    to receive their legacy in paradise.

GOD Most blessed was the hour that you were born,°
    Lady, this you must not doubt.
    What pleases you is what my heart desires.   1840
    Blessed was the hour that you begot me,
    and suckled me and nourished me.
    I love you as much as my own heart,
    my dear mother, dear sister.
    Do not be disheartened,   1845
    your crown is already prepared°
    and will soon be on your head.
    I grant you paradise as your fief:
    All those who have served you
    and who adored you in the world,   1850
    and all the virtuous shall I place in glory.
    But as for the wicked, I could not
    in all justice prevent them from being damned:
    It was an evil hour that they were ever born from Adam.
    I shall show them my countenance—   1855
    I who for them suffered such ignominy—
    And the manner of my crucifixion.

1830 The identification of the speaker, presumably given on the missing folio, is lost, but it clearly is the Virgin Mary, who has been addressed by the kings, Cherubim and Seraphim, and the saints, and who now addresses Jesus Christ directly as her Son (l. 1830) and recalls her sorrow at the Crucifixion (ll. 1830–31; cf. John 19:25). The dramatis personae lists "Mére de Dieu" (fol. 1ᵛ) as a character. Mary is often shown interceding with her Son in Last Judgment plays; see, for example, *Le Jugement Dernier (Lo Jutgamen General)*, 138–41, ll. 1356–96.

1838–41 Christ's blessings on his mother echo the "Magnificat" spoken by Mary after the Annunciation (cf. Luke 1:48); it is a canticle recited daily at Vespers.

1846–48 Christ alludes to the Coronation of the Virgin (cf. ll. 1734–36). Following the procedures of feudal custom, Christ gives Mary Heaven as her fief.

In this way the good will be edified,
while the wicked will tremble
and wail pitifully   1860
as a result of their failure to be redeemed
by such a very precious treasure.
Their abode will be in Hell.
Get up, John, the moment has come
to accomplish what we have to do.   1865
Go on, eradicate the world°
and engulf it in fire and flames,
for it is filled to overflowing with great infamy.
I do not wish to delay any longer.

SAINT JOHN THE EVANGELIST We must bow down to you,   1870
and will carry out your orders.
At this point we will not rest
until your will is accomplished.
The earth has been incinerated and destroyed.
The world is now eradicated.   1875

GOD John, Luke, Mark, and Matthew,°
my four special ministers
who are otherwise known as the Evangelists,
get up without any further delay,
and go off instantly to blow your trumpets°   1880
in the four corners of the world,
to the farthest reaches of the globe.
Bring the dead back to life
and make souls once again reside in their bodies,
from which they have been separated.   1885

1866–67 Christ, seated in judgment, now commands John the Evangelist to destroy the world, an unusual interpretation of the biblical account (cf. Apoc. 19:20, 20:9, and 20:14), where John simply watches the destruction of evil by fire and brimstone. How the destruction is staged is not clear, but it has taken place by l. 1874.

1876 The Four Evangelists are named in the reverse order in which their gospels appear in the New Testament.

1880–95 Although in the biblical account the trumpets that raise the dead are given to angels (Matt. 24:31), in the play the Four Evangelists are given trumpets and sent into the four ends of the earth. This eschatological event, which concludes the history of the Church, may allude to Christ's final command after the Resurrection, in which he commissions his disciples as missionaries (Matt. 28:19) to establish the Church. Other possible explanations for the role of the Evangelists as trumpeters are suggested by *Jour du Jugement*, ed. Roy, 55–58. Miniature 76, placed at the end of God's speech, pictures Christ enthroned and instructing the Four Evangelists, each of whom holds a trumpet.

John, you shall go to the expanses
of the East, and Matthew will go
to the West, where he will decree
that all beings will, through true resurrection,°
come to judgment.   1890
And you, Mark, shall proclaim
the resurrection in the lands of the north.
Luke, you shall go toward the south
and do just as I have instructed the others.
Each of you, take your trumpet.   1895

SAINT JOHN THE EVANGELIST Not a single one will stop
  before it is done according to your directive.
  Rise up without any resistance,°
  you bodies that have lain beneath the earth.
  Each and every one of you, get yourselves ready,   1900
  body and soul together,
  for I must assemble you
  all in order to lead you to the judgment
  of the sovereign King who tells no lies.
  Get up, for I am calling you.   1905

SAINT MATTHEW° I bring you the announcement,
  you who were rotting in the ground,
  that you must come forth from your sepulchers
  and assume once more both body and soul.
  Those who have lived without blame   1910
  will be in everlasting joy—
  this is neither a lie nor a fabrication—
  and the wicked will all in total abjection
  be cast down to Hell.
  Get up, you have slept more than enough.   1915

SAINT MARK° You are about to receive a jolt from me,
  you bodies that are lying in this earth;

1889 The emphasis on true resurrection is intended to contrast with the pseudo-resurrection faked earlier by Antichrist (cf. l. 792).

1898 John now addresses the dead directly. To fulfill Christ's instructions, he and the other Evangelists probably move across stage taking positions in opposite corners.

1906 Matthew is symbolized by the winged man, one of the four living creatures that surround the throne of God (Apoc. 4:7–8). For the medieval understanding of Matthew, see Jacobus de Voragine, *Golden Legend*, 2:183–88.

1916 Mark is symbolized by the winged lion, another of the four living creatures (Apoc. 4:7–8). See Jacobus de Voragine, *Golden Legend*, 1:242–48.

I have come looking for all of you.
By true resurrection,
all of you around here arise,   1920
both in body and soul; wait
no longer, for it has been commanded by God.
He who has done good will find himself fulfilled,
and he who has done evil will pay.
You must come to judgment.   1925

SAINT LUKE° Death can hold you no longer,
    you bodies who have gone its way:
    Arise, surely you weary
    of lying down here in the earth.
    Get up now, make no further delay,   1930
    all of you take back your souls
    and come off with me
    to the judgment of the All Powerful.
    The good will most assuredly be apprised
    of the virtuous deeds they have performed in their lives,   1935
    and the wicked will not at all
    be spared from the consequences of their evil.

BISHOP° Alas! What a shame I was born!
    What a shame I was ever an archdeacon!
    Over there I see people blacker than soot°   1940
    who will receive us in their troop.
    Things have started out badly:
    I treated myself to so much comfort in the world
    that now my body and soul together
    will have all the misery.   1945
    My entire body is trembling with fear,

1926 Luke is symbolized by the winged ox, another of the four living creatures
(Apoc. 4:7–8). See Jacobus de Voragine, *Golden Legend*, 2:247–54.

1938 The Bishop is probably the Evil Bishop who converted to Antichrist earlier
and suggested that he raise the dead (ll. 744–67). The Bishop introduces the next
category of speakers traditional in Last Judgment plays, evil men and women of all
classes and callings who recognize upon their resurrection from the dead that they are
ill prepared to face their judge. Their complaints often allude to vices and sins that
were considered typical of their professions and that were castigated in reformist and
satirical literature. *Lo Jutgamen General* (see *Le Jugement Dernier*, 94–116, ll. 643–975),
for example, emphasizes the judgment on and punishment of various religious orders
and secular classes.

1940 Blacker than soot: MS "plus noirs que tacres." The Bishop recognizes the
devils waiting to take the damned to Hell.

for I see quite distinctly
how I acted in this world.
I neglected to instruct my people;
I abandoned them for the magnificent courts   1950
of princes, dukes, and kings,
on account of whom I committed many foolish deeds
and imposed such onerous tithes.

ABBESS Lord bishop, I as well,°
Alas! What a pitiful creature! I am damned   1955
because of the life we led,
you and I, in this putrid world.
Now we shall be relegated to the deep
pit of Hell and never get back out again.
It would have been much better for me never   1960
to have been born than to live in misery.
I wish I had never been born.
We must go to our judgment.

AGOULANT *king*°
Alas! Why did I act this way?
On earth I was a king with a crown.
I completely abdicated my responsibilities   1965
by giving nothing and forever taking.
I did not choose to put any effort into good works,
and I treated the poor with scorn.

THE BAILIFF° I must arise without any delay.   1970
I can already see my condemnation:
Never was it my intention to do anything
but grab and pilfer.
I caused more than a thousand men to be hanged
out of hatred and for the sake of gifts.   1975

THE PROVOST Alas! I am far removed from any pardon.
I can easily see that I too have failed.

1954–57 Roy (*Jour du Jugement,* 20) suggests that the Abbess may have had a lover,
the "riche clerc" listed in the dramatis personae, but these lines imply that her lover
is the Bishop.

after 1963 Agoulant is one of the kings who converted to Antichrist (ll. 1010–13),
but who, unlike the other kings (ll. 1676–92), did not later repent. Along with other
dead bodies, Agoulant, still wearing his crown (cf. l. 1965), is pictured rising from the
grave in min. 79, placed in the MS at the end of his speech.

1970 The Bailiff is the first to appear of three civil officers who have abused their
authority, hurting others for their own personal gain.

Many people have been on numerous occasions
mistreated and looted because of me,
and many others hanged and murdered.   1980
I plundered wrongly and without any sanction.

THE LAWYER As for me, many times did I deceive
in order to acquire temporal goods
which are worth little—this I know
all too well, for I was a lawyer.   1985
I took in lots of money then,
but none of it is worth so much as a wooden stick.
I took on many a case
that was fraudulent and evil.

THE QUEEN I am suffering because of my pride.   1990
I was too haughty,
disdainful, and lustful,
and destroyed my marriage.
Pain and fury are stabbing at my heart.
I see now that I was terribly naive   1995
in so indulging my fancies
when I lived in the world.

THE MISER° I was avaricious,
hostile, and full of resentment.
Not for anything in the world would I have given a   2000
penny for the sake of Our Lord,
and I will undergo enormous pain because of it.
Alas! Now I don't know what to say.

THE USURER° I ought to curse the day and the hour

1998 MS "L'avaricieux," the avaricious. Unlike the others who are raised from the
dead, the Miser is a character type rather than a member of a profession or class; he
particularly represents the uncharitable (ll. 2000–1). Last Judgment plays often portray
such character types (e.g., the glutton, lecher, hypocrite). *Lo Jutgamen General* (see *Le
Jugement Dernier*, 164–218, ll. 1825–2698), for example, includes representatives of all
seven deadly sins, each accompanied by a corresponding devil; similarly, the Italian
L'Anticristo e il Giudizio Finale stages characters representing the deadly sins, hypocrisy, and blasphemy. The Chur *Last Judgment* links some of these sins to Antichrist, who
is shown speaking with Pride, Avarice, Lust, Wrath, and Gluttony; see *Churer
Weltgerichstspiel*, ed. Schulze, 91–92.

2004 The play particularly stresses the punishment of usury, the practice of charg-
ing interest on money, which was considered sinful in the Middle Ages (cf. ll. 2064–
69). Not only the Usurer but also his entire household is condemned. On the play's
treatment of usury, see *Jour du Jugement*, ed. Roy, 63–66. Two miniatures illustrate this
scene. Miniature 80, placed in the MS after l. 2029, shows the Usurer and his house-

73

that I was ever of woman born. 2005
Today, in body and in soul,
I shall be condemned to Hell.

THE USURER'S WIFE Pitiful wretch, what am I to do?
What a shame that I got mixed up with usury.
It is in Hell, full of corruption, 2010
that I shall have to remain forever more.

THE USURER'S NURSE I am heading toward God, the celestial King,
who will today render justice to all people.
Alas! What a painful duty this is!
When I was in the usurer's household, 2015
I suckled their child with the milk of my own breasts
and served as its nursemaid.
Alas! I acted pretty foolishly,
for I was quite aware of the truth,
that what I had to eat and drink 2020
came from the profits of money-lending.

THE USURER'S CHILD Alas! in what sorrow I was begotten!
What an anguishing birth!
For God, who wields total power,
will judge me today. 2025
He will certainly remember, this I am sure of,
that I was nourished by usury,
and I shall undergo intense suffering because of it.
I do not know what will happen to my soul.

GOD Usurer, the Devil will lead you away 2030
and you will go straight to Hell
when you withdraw from my presence,
for by all rights you have earned it.
When you would see an amputee,
or poverty-stricken children, men, and women, 2035
or people with paralyzed arms, feet, or legs,
no matter how crippled they were,
never did they receive from you the slightest relief—
not so much as a single meal from your stock of food—
although they asked you 2040
in my name and that of my mother.

---

hold rising from their coffins, while Christ judges them; and min. 81, placed after l.
2075, shows them being led to Hell by the devil Hazart.

THE USURER Woe is me! How I am paying for
    those great possessions, those immense riches,
    the elegant and noble entourage,
    my great florins and my deniers,°   2045
    the wheat I kept in my granges,
    and in which I took such delight.
    Now there is nothing to give me pleasure
    in all this; never will I be worth anything.
    I shall go off with the devils   2050
    and burn forever more without any respite.

GOD When you would hear the poor lament,
    they who in my name asked you for bread
    and waited long hours for your alms
    in the rain, the cold, and violent weather,   2055
    you allowed them to die like animals
    at your door, without making any donation.
    Come here, you miserable wretch,
    wicked and foul creature:
    You have at all times abided in usury.   2060
    Nothing did you wish to give on my account
    no matter how many pleas and entreaties
    the beggars would make to you,
    and yet you have often heard the teachings°
    of those who know the Scripture,   2065
    namely that all those who live by usury
    and take others' goods without giving anything back
    would be sent down to Hell by me
    because of the goods they had amassed.
    You neglected my command   2070
    and lived by usury,
    all four of you, this you all know well.
    Body and soul together, each as a complete individual,
    I hereby give the four of you to the Devil.
    Over here, Hazart, I am handing them over to you.   2075

HAZART *devil*
    Spring forward—are you tipsy?—°

2045 Florins were gold coins originally associated with the international banking
firms of Florence; deniers were smaller, less valuable coins, like pennies.

2064–67 Cf. Deut. 23:19; Proverbs 28:8.

2076–80 Hazart immediately addresses the Usurer and his household. He ironically
describes their punishment in Hell as a levy, a kind of usury based upon what they

into the thundering chasm of Hell.
Here I shall levy upon you the tax
that you have long owed me
for the goods you possessed in the world.   2080
You can feed yourselves on the fire and the lightning—
you have indeed found a good master in me.
The cauldron is already prepared.

BEELZEBUB *devil*
    I am going to place your head
    and your entire body into it.   2085
    Take a look, pal, I ask if you ever
    saw such beautiful prey
    as these usurers. I request
    you to arrange for them to be served.

AGRAPPART *devil*
    I am well aware that they have deserved   2090
    to have an ample share of Hell.
    I shall place them in the zone°
    where the lightning is most torrid,
    for many a good man has been reduced to poverty
    by their racket.   2095

THE BISHOP I have no doubt, in truth, that the Devil
    will carry me off today,
    and no one will ever bring me consolation for it.
    I was lord and overseer
    of a bishopric, as well as a feared leader   2100
    of all men:
    I was well heeded by worthy clerks,
    by princes and prelates,
    but now I am totally gone astray. Alas!
    What a pitiful creature I am!   2105
    I spent my time on lascivious affairs,
    so many days that they are without number.
    The archenemy, who subjugates people,

---

have long owed the Devil. As early as the mid second century, the *Apocalypse of Peter*
describes money lenders and usurers being punished in Hell, as does the later *Apocalypse of Paul*; see Gardiner, *Visions of Heaven and Hell,* 8, 39.
    2092 Medieval belief, especially developed in popular accounts, understood Hell to
be divided into various zones or, as in Dante's *Inferno,* circles, each with punishments
appropriate to the sins of the damned condemned to the area.

deceived me while I was alive.
Without deserving them I received 2110
revenues from the Holy Church.
Alas! How pathetic I am to realize only too late
that I deserved them not a whit.
I was too much the slave of the devils,
doing everything they wished, 2115
so much did they tempt me in the course of my life.
I lost God, my creator,
whenever I saw an attractive woman,°
it didn't matter whether she was a religious or a maiden,
a bourgeois, a noble lady, or a young girl, 2120
a holy nun or a beguine,°
even if she held a high and honorable office,
as a provisioner, a prioress, or an abbess.°
Many a time did I for this reason skip out on mass,
in order to gaze at a beautiful lady. 2125
At that point, any precautions were useless:
I could not be prevented from having my way with
her body, and sleeping with her,
no matter how virtuous she tried to be.

PRIORESS What a sorrowful wretch I am! Who would ever
have imagined 2130
that I would receive such a reward
for my sin? Not for any possessions

2118–29 The Bishop here plays the role of the insatiable lecher. His interest in all women, whether aristocratic or middle class, virgins or ladies, young or old, secular or religious, is emphasized. He is later accused by the Prioress (ll. 2146–50).

2121 MS "nonnain sacree, nonnain benigne." Although the line may be rendered, "a holy nun, a blessed nun," given the force of the Bishop's complaint—which lists as many types of women as possible—we believe the reference is to a beguine. In the later Middle Ages some traced the etymology of *beguine* to *benignitas*, a view rejected by Gautier de Coincy; see Robert Lerner, *Heresy of the Free Spirit in the Later Middle Ages* (Berkeley: Univ. of California Press, 1972), 39. Nuns were members of monastic institutions who took vows comparable to those taken by monks. Beguines, though not in monastic orders, were members of sisterhoods who served the sick and poor and emphasized manual work. Ironically, given the Bishop's lust, both groups of women took vows of chastity.

2123 An abbess governed a convent of nuns; a prioress governed a priory, which was often subordinate to an abbey or convent. Both hold high-ranking ecclesiastical positions. Their illicit association with the Bishop is suggested in two miniatures: in the first, placed in the MS before l. 1954, the Bishop is shown rising from the dead with the Abbess; the second, placed after l. 2129, shows him accompanied by the Prioress.

that anyone might have offered to me
would I have given over
my body to the sin of lust.   2135
Forever more I shall wallow in the scorching heat
of hellfire and its flames,
of this I am sure, both body and soul.
For the rest of my days it will go on without respite,
as long as God wishes, and without respite   2140
will I continue this penitence.
Dear God, who will, by your sentence,
judge me this very day,
I know very well that you will regard me
with bitterness and extend no mercy.   2145
Lord bishop, your friendship
and the love that you showed me
when you joined with me carnally
and became my lover:
It is this love that has put me in Hell.   2150
The devils will be my ministers.
I am sure of this, for the Four Evangelists
have summoned all mortal bodies here;
now my sin can remain hidden
no longer, and I don't know what to do   2155
when I gaze into the eyes of Jesus Christ.°

· ·

SAINT MARK Get up once and for all, for you will receive
        no more
    deferrals; you must come
    to the great court, and submit
    to the judgment of God, the true judge   2160
    who adjudicates everything equitably.

---

after 2156 A folio is lost here. The missing passage probably staged further speeches by the damned, perhaps including the knights, who played such important roles
earlier in the play, and the Jews, who are addressed later by the Angel holding the
lance (cf. l. 2209). It may also have included a character listed in the dramatis personae but missing from the play as extant, the Rich Clerk (fol. 1ʳ). It probably also
included speeches by John and Matthew; the resurrected damned have been respond-
ing to the trumpets sounded by the Four Evangelists, and speeches by Mark and Luke
begin the next extant folio.

Get going, for you have delayed too long.

SAINT LUKE Run quickly to Judgment.
You can put it off no longer,
of this I am sure: The moment will no more be delayed   2165
when the Judge will come to take his place.
He will want to see each and every one of you.
He will judge each one according to his works.
There is not a single creature that can hide°
what has been done before his face.   2170

GOD It is now the time for me
to display my insignia to all people.°
It is this that teaches everyone
how my people put me
to death—I who was their friend—   2175
and how I, God, chose to come down from Heaven
for their sake and hang on the cross.
I wish to show it so that everyone should look upon it:
No better sustenance could I offer them.
Now all of you give me your undivided attention: 2180
I am Jesus Christ, your King,
who in order to redeem you from Hell
allowed my body to be struck and beaten.
I was sold for thirty deniers°
and was hanged on the cross for you.   2185
In my side and in my hip
they wounded me with this lance,
so that the blood flowed down to my feet.
I was fastened with these nails
and yet it was not because of any sin of mine,   2190

2169–70 MS: "N'est nulle chose qui se meure / Ce qui est fait devant sa face." The
passage is difficult, but its force is that no evil act, no matter how awful or secret, can
be kept from God.

2172 Christ's insignia are the tokens of his Crucifixion. In addition to the five
wounds—nail marks on his hands and feet and the cut in his side made by the lance
of the Roman soldier (John 19:34), named Longinus in medieval legend—the insignia
also include the instruments of his Passion: the nails used to bind Christ to the cross,
which he may hold while he speaks (l. 2189), and the cross (l. 2177) and lance (l.
2187), which are held by the two angels who speak next. Christ's speech, emphasizing
his bodily suffering (ll. 2172–89), reflects the concerns of later medieval spirituality;
contemporary art similarly encouraged veneration of the cross by vividly portraying
the bloody, bruised, and twisted body of Christ.

2184 deniers (cf. l. 2045). In the biblical account Judas sold Jesus for thirty pieces of
silver (Matt. 26:15).

but rather because of Adam who ate
the fruit that was forbidden.
I suffered great hunger and thirst,
meager lodging and extreme poverty,
yet not a single person opened his house to me   2195
nor did me any but the most paltry good turn.
No one wants to believe in my name any more:
Even children have contested me,
taken my name in vain and repudiated me.
They will come to repentance too late.   2200
You good people, gather over to one side,°
for I wish to take vengeance upon the wicked.

ANGEL *with cross, in song*°
All of you come to hear the sentence
of the Lord, the gentle and benevolent King.
Do you see here present the sign°   2205
whereupon he suffered his death and passion
for your redemption,
you at least who have deserved it?

ANGEL *with lance*
Treacherous Jews, now you know
how he was mutilated by you   2210
and fastened with these three nails°
to that cross and hanged high above,
and how his side was pierced

2201 Christ now separates the good resurrected from the evil, who have been dreading their judgment. Probably following the usual pattern for the separation of "the sheep from the goats" (cf. Matt. 25:32–33), the good move to Christ's right, whereas the evil wait on his left.

after 2202 MS "Anges de la croix en chant." The Angel's song (ll. 2203–8) is set to music that, according to Roy (*Jour du Jugement*, 15), resembles *Urbs Jerusalem beata;* but see the discussion of its music in Appendix 3, below. Min 83, placed in the MS just above this rubric, pictures Christ seated in judgment. He reveals his wounds, while two angels above him hold the cross and the lance, and the resurrected kneel below.

2205 The Angel stresses the presence of the tokens in the sight of those judged, and therefore in the sight of the audience. A similar emphasis is evident again in the lines spoken by the next angel.

2211–19 The Second Angel again displays the tokens of the Passion, probably taking the nails earlier held by Christ (cf. l. 2189). In addition to displaying the lance (l. 2214), the Angel also points to the crown of thorns (ll. 2215–16), which was forced on the head of Jesus when he was mocked (Matt. 27:29), and to the vessel (ll. 2217–19)—often a sponge—used to give Jesus wine mixed with gall (Matt. 27:34) and vinegar (Matt. 27:48).

for your sake by this mighty lance.
Here present is the crown   2215
with which you crowned the gentle King
and the vessel in which you gave
to the all-powerful and divine King
bitter poison and sour wine to drink.
He will give you your recompense for it.   2220

GOD My disciples, each of you will come°
    and take his place at the Judgment,
    and I will have you look upon all those
    who despised you in the world
    and who hated you in my name.   2225
    You have always remained with me,
    through winter and through summer,
    in all my temptations.°
    By you the twelve tribes°
    of Israel I wish you to judge,   2230
    just as I said when you were with me
    in the world, where you had nothing but travail.
    Come with me down there
    and render final judgment.

SAINT PETER Flee, o cursed ones, how misguided you were°   2235
    when you indulged in pleasures of the flesh,
    for this does not at all suit the Judge:
    He is no longer willing to tolerate it.
    Forever more in foul and putrid sulphur
    shall you burn, with no respite.   2240

SAINT PAUL You miserable creatures, no longer can you put off
    going to the furnace
    of Hell, which is so exceedingly repugnant,
    and where you shall forever more be beaten:
    God has squashed your pride.   2245
    Take yourselves over to the left-hand side.

2221–25 "Know you not that the saints shall judge this world?" (1 Cor. 6:2). Cf. Matt. 5:10–12.

2228 The line is unclear. We read MS "temptacïons," amending Roy's "templacïons."

2229–30 For the twelve tribes of Israel, see Apoc. 7:4–8.

2235–46 Peter and Paul now judge the evil, directing them to God's left (l. 2246); cf. note to l. 2201.

SAINT ANDREW And you others, you who have served the King,°
    go over to the right,
    for you have deserved this respite
    and you will indeed have it; and it will be without end.   2250
    Never a single day shall you be assaulted
    by the enemy, your adversary.°

SAINT JAMES The All Powerful will be magnanimous
    to you, the blessed.
    You can be sure that he is aware   2255
    of the good deeds that you have performed for him.
    You did well, and now you should know°
    that since you have served a great Lord,
    you shall have a reward greater
    than you could possibly imagine.   2260

SAINT MATTHEW As for you, poisonous scoundrels,°
    go on over that way, like the prisoners you are.
    When God called at your door°
    you deigned not open up to him;
    nor when he was naked did you offer   2265
    to cover him. You did not even obey
    his command. Tell me why
    he should have mercy on you now.

SAINT PHILIP Don't have a sad or gloomy heart,
    you who left the world for God's sake,   2270
    and who followed after him,
    maintaining absolute poverty.°
    The deeds you did for him
    will be recounted before the Judge.

SAINT BARTHOLOMEW Wretches, go to that place
    you all know about.   2275
    You certainly know where you must go.
    You must plummet to Hell,

2247–60 Andrew and James judge the saved, directing them to God's right (l. 2248); cf. note to l. 2201.

2252 The adversary is the Devil (cf. 1 Peter 5:8).

2257 You did well: MS "Belles feistes."

2261–88 Matthew now begins a series of speeches by the saints, which are addressed in alternating sequence first to the damned and then to the saved.

2263–66 Cf. Matt. 25:43.

2272 Cf. Matt. 10:9–10.

for that is to be your inheritance.
Now you shall pay for your excesses,
your ostentation, and your opulence.   2280
From now on you shall have nothing but misery
and every kind of misfortune.

SAINT JAMES THE GREATER° Your purity will illuminate you,
who have kept your flesh unsullied
by any filthy stains.   2285
Because of it, you shall be crowned in Heaven.
Go to the right where God has ordained
a spot for every just person.

SAINT THOMAS° You were excessively covetous on earth,
envious and miserly in the extreme.   2290
Now you cannot cleanse yourselves
of your sins, which have overtaken you,
and which have wounded you to the heart.
Go along with these foul devils.

SAINT THADDEUS° You placed all your efforts   2295
into pleasantries, lies, and fables,
into games and jests,
and into misdeeds and slander.
Never did you maintain the Ten
Commandments of the perfect King   2300
who now is causing everything to quake.°
This is why you will be damned without redemption.

SAINT SIMON It won't do you any good to put up a dispute,
knaves. Now the time has come
for you to receive   2305
the recompense for your misdeeds.
The mouth of Hell is open°
for you, felons, of this you can be sure,

2283 MS "Saint Jasque le grant." Another name for James, the brother of John, who
has spoken just above (ll. 2253–60). He is called "the Greater" to distinguish him from
James the Less, a relative of Jesus. See Jacobus de Voragine, *Golden Legend*, 1:269–77.

2289 Thomas, the doubting disciple (John 20:25), became a missionary to India. He
may hold his attribute, a builder's square. See Jacobus de Voragine, *Golden Legend*,
1:29–35.

2295 Thaddeus was one of the original twelve disciples of Jesus (cf. Matt. 10:3).

2301 Cf. Apoc. 16:18.

2307 In medieval art and drama, Hell is often represented as a set of huge gaping
jaws. See Pamela Sheingorn, "'Who Can Open the Doors of His Face?'" 1–19.

83

in order to receive both body and soul.
Never will you have a single day's respite. 2310

GOD The time has come to render the sentence.
Come forward, blessed ones.
You are pure of all evil.
Look upon my Father's kingdom.
Henceforth I wish it to be made open to you. 2315
Some time ago I set it up for you;°
it has been prepared for you
since the beginning of the world:
You are all unblemished by sin.
Never will you be able to sin even an instant. 2320
Everything you wish will be accomplished
and you will have everlasting joy.
The devils no longer have any power over you.
When I was hungry, you gave me to eat;°
when I was thirsty, you gave me to drink; 2325
when I was cold, you covered me;
when I was in prison, full of sorrow,
you gave me consolation and joy;
and when I sought shelter from you
you gave it to me gladly. 2330
This is why my Father
has granted to you his holy paradise.

THE JUST MAN° When did we see you, how long ago,°
at our home? When did we shelter you?
When did we console you in your prison? 2335
When was it that we saw you
and clothed you?
When was it that you were hungry and thirsty,
only to be nourished by us?
Tell us this, by your noble character. 2340

GOD Gladly.

2316–18 Cf. Matt. 25:34.

2324–39 Cf. Matt. 25:35–36.

2333 MS "Li Justes." Although the speaker represents all the righteous saved and speaks in the plural, the role is probably played by one actor. The dramatis personae lists "Li justes hom" (fol. 1ʳ) as a character. His role is analogous to that of "li bons crestiens" (after l. 1423); in both cases these good characters are treated almost as personifications representing entire classes.

2333–40 Cf. Matt. 25:37–39.

THE JUST Tell us the story now,
please, by your abundant friendship.

GOD When you took pity on the poor,°
you necessarily took pity on me as well.
You are blessed and were blessed,   2345
for all the good things that you did for them
and all the good that you said to them
were without any doubt done also for me.

THE JUST May you be praised in all your perfection
for having so marvelously protected us!   2350

GOD Wretched ones, away with you, delay no longer!°
Into the eternal fires of Hell, ever blazing,
tarry no more:
Go to your everlasting torment.
At no time will you ever be able to achieve   2355
a state of salvation;
rather shall you remain forever in flames,
without end and without redemption,
in the dark prison of Hell.
When you saw me hungry,°   2360
near death, you did not feed me;
when I was thirsty, you brought me no aid;
when I was naked, your hard hearts
refused me your clothing,
so deep was your arrogance.   2365
You left me in prison,
for you did not deign
to offer me comfort or consolation.
Go on now, without any succor,
to that painful misery for the rest of your days.   2370

THE LAWYER° This sentence is exceptionally cruel

2343–48 Cf. Matt. 25:40.
2351–54 Cf. Matt. 25:41.
2360–68 Cf. Matt. 25:42–43.
2371 Whereas all the righteous saved are represented by the Just Man, the damned
are more specifically differentiated. In addition to the Lawyer, some of the other evil
characters who spoke after their resurrection, such as Agoulant, the Bailiff, and the
Queen (ll. 1964–97), probably speak on the missing folio following l. 2379. The missing
folio may also have included speeches by the Queen's Ladies listed in the dramatis
personae (fol. 1ʳ) but missing from the play. In any case, the Queen is already on her
way to Hell (ll. 2380–81) when the action resumes on the next extant folio.

to us; can we not make an appeal?
When you came looking for shelter°
we were not aware of it in our house.
Do tell us how many times   2375
we refused or declined
to give you food or drink.
Never were you a single day in prison,
as far as we knew.

. . . .

THE QUEEN Alas! How ruthless you are,   2380
  you devil, to be carrying me like this!°

RAPILLART *devil*°
  Princes of Hell, open your doors!°
  Don't you see our masters who are coming here
  and leading with them in captivity
  their prisoners, weighted down in chains?°   2385
  Come outside, hurry forth.
  Make sure to give them plenty of misery.
  We have received our sentence:
  Never will we have any additional ones.°

2373–79 Cf. Matt. 25:44. The missing folio probably included Christ's answer, based on Matt. 25:45–46: "Then he shall answer them, saying: Amen I say to you, as long as you did it not to one of these least, neither did you do it to me. And these shall go into everlasting punishment: but the just, into life everlasting."

2381 The Queen is probably carried over the devil's back, which is how medieval art and drama often show the damned being taken to Hell.

after 2381 Rapillart's name—probably derived from a conflation of two common nouns, *rapine* (rape, plunder) and *piller* (to pillage)—suggests plunderer, robber. A tenth devil, Rapillart is not included in the demonic council early in the play (ll. 193–253). The ten devils may be intended to contrast to the nine orders of angels and to recall the ten circles of Dante's *Inferno*.

2382 Rapillart's challenge echoes the words attributed to Christ during the Harrowing of Hell, which are based on Psalm 23 [KJ=24]: 7–10. See Russell, *Lucifer*, 106–08.

2385 Medieval art and drama often portray devils leading the damned to Hell in chains.

2389 The Last Judgment determines the full membership of the damned (cf. ll. 2399–2400, 2404–5), since the righteous are taken to Heaven and there will be no further opportunity for devils to tempt or for humans to sin. Miniature 88, placed in the MS following this line, pictures Rapillart leading a very large group of the damned to the gates of Hell, where they are met by Belial.

BELIAL *devil*

    Rapillart, you certainly are aware 2390
    that we have been apprised of this.
    Believe me, we saw
    all the dead being resurrected;
    we had to expel ours
    from here. I have no idea 2395
    to whom we can appeal, and even the sea
    listened to God's messenger
    and likewise gave up its dead.°
    I know indeed that we will never have any more.

HAZART *devil*

    What you say is true, for there are no more of them 2400
    and the world has come to an end.
    But let our entire effort
    be devoted to torturing these ones forever,
    for we will never be allowed the slightest possibility
    of capturing any others; 2405
    this is why we must concentrate
    on doubling the torment of these pitiful ones.

THE USURER Alas! What sorrow! Alas! Alas!
    I have been dispatched to the eternal presence
    of the king of every iniquity,° 2410
    and shall be toasted on every side.

SAINT JOHN Over here will be your quarters,°
    holy people, all of you are of royal stature.
    Never shall you suffer any ill,°
    hunger or thirst, misfortune or discomfort, 2415
    never shall you see or think
    anything that you find displeasing.
    Forever more shall you be joyous

2398 "And the sea gave up the dead that were in it, and death and hell gave up their dead that were in them; and they were judged every one according to their works" (Apoc. 20:13).

2410 MS "Dou Roy de toute iniquite."

2412–34 The play concludes with the speeches of John, Luke, and Paul. The saved are directed toward the gates of Heaven (l. 2412) and invited to praise God (ll. 2422–27), whereas the damned and the devils, now offstage, are simply alluded to in passing (ll. 2430–35). The last miniature, placed in the MS after John's speech, shows the three saints addressing the saved.

2414–17 Cf. Apoc. 21:4.

and filled with grace;
you shall look upon God's countenance°   2420
and be even more favored than the angels.

SAINT LUKE Let us all praise him:
He who is, who was, and who will be,°
he who will shelter you herein
and through whom you have vanquished   2425
the devils, and have achieved glory
everlasting.
We will forever be his kin°
and never will take our leave.

SAINT PAUL Lords, the devils   2430
have departed, and taken
the souls with them
to Hell; there will they be
tortured forever,
more than anything in the world.   2435
And we shall have joy.
Let us now sing *Te Deum*°
with ringing voices.

Amen, Amen.°

2420 Cf. Apoc. 22:4.
2423 Cf. Apoc. 1:4, 8.
2428 Cf. 2 Cor. 6:18.
2437 *Te Deum [laudamus]:* We give praise to God. The canticle sung at the conclusion of Sunday Matins, it is a traditional ending for many medieval plays. For the
music see *Liber Usualis,* 1832–34.
after 2438 *Amen* is the concluding word of the Christian Bible (cf. Apoc. 22:21).

Appendices

Appendix 1: Sample Text from Besançon 579

The following two passages newly transcribed and edited from Besançon 579 will allow readers to compare the translation with the original Middle French text. The relatively few abbreviations in the manuscript have been resolved and printed in italics. Proper names have been capitalized. Punctuation has been added, as well as diacritical marks, including a trema to denote vowels in hiatus having a full syllable count. All word divisions of the manuscript have been respected, with the exception of lines 378 (atelle), 384 (couchaige), 408 (prente), 538 (atoy), 561 (atoy), 568 (adelivre), and 590 (lamer). Line numbers corresponding to the translation and folio placement are included in the right-hand column. The latter portion of the first passage, lines 430–55, corresponds to the photographic reproduction of fol. 8^v.

I. Birth of Antichrist and Visitation of the Devils:
lines 366–455 (episodes 6–8)

MERE ANTRECRIST Ha, ennemis,   [fol. 7^r, col. b]
   que ne m'en portes,
   Qui ainssinques m'as assotee,
   Quar grosse d'enfant m'as laissiee!
   Or ne say je que devenir;
   Bien vourroie ma vie fenir,   370
   Que je ne say que puisse faire.

   [Miniature No. 10]   [fol. 7^v, col. a]

LA DAMOISELLE Ma douce dame debonnaire,
   Par amours ne vous esmaiez;
   En vous bon reconfort ayez,
   Et vostre duel laissiez aler: 375
   Vous n'y povez riens conquester.
   Aiez en vous bonne esperance,
   Quar Mahons a telle puissance,
   Bien de cecy vous puet aidier.

MERE ANTRECRIST Douce amye, tant ne plaidier: 380
   Tu ne sanz pas le mal que sen.
   Par po que je n'is hors dou san
   Quant j'osay faire tel oultraige
   Qu'avec le deable me couchai ge.
   Ce fu mout grant forçonnerie,   385
   Mais pour tant ne m'en repen mie,
   Quar bien say que mes filz doit estre
   Plus puissans quë hons nez n'a nestre: [fol. 7ᵛ, col. b]
   C'est tout ce qui me reconforte.
   Par li yert Crestïenté morte   390
   Et Juïf seront relevé.

LA DAMOISSELLE Ma dame, plus vous est levé
   Le ventre qu'il n'iere avant hier.
   Je lo que parmy se santier
   En aliens en celle maison: 395
   De vous gisir sera saison
   Partans, g'en suis toute certainne.

MERE ANTRECRIST Ma tres douce suer, or m'y moinne!
   Il me tarde mout que g'i soye,
   De repos bon mestier avroie.   400
   Or en alons, ma douce amie!

LA DAMOISELLE Dame, de vostre compaignie
   Suis je mout liee et mot joians;
   Il me tarde nous y soiens
   Pour vous aidier et conforter.   405

MERE ANTRECRIST Ma suer, plus ne me puis porter.
   Lasse doulante, lasse moy!
   Ma suer, pren te garde de moy: [fol. 8ʳ, col. a]
   Je san es costez trop grant raige.
   Lasse doulente, que feray je?   410
   Bien croi que g'en perdrai la vie.

   [Miniature No. 11]

LA DAMOISELLE Dame, ne vous esmaiez mie,
   Quar Mahomet vous aydera
   Et bien tost vous delivrera.
   Certes, bien tost acoucherez   415
   Et d'enfant delivre serez.

Dame, un biau fil avez sanz doubte.

[Miniature No. 12]

MERE ANTRECRIST Je met m'esperance trestoute [fol. 8ʳ, col. b]
En Mahon *et* en sa puissance.
Fol sont trestuit cil sanz doubtance   420
Qui ne croient ces vertuz belles.

AGRAPPART DEABLE Seigneur, je vous aport nouvelles,
Quar Entrecriz est nez en terre.
Nous pourrons des ormés *con*querre
Trestouz les crestïens dou monde.   425

[Miniature No. 13]

PLUTO DEABLE Li maux feux d'enfer les confonde!
Si vrayement co*m*me il me tarde
Quë en enfer trestouz les arde!
De riens ne seroie plus aise.

SATAM DEABLE Hasart, je te pri qu'il te plaise [fol. 8ᵛ, col. a] 430
Quë entre toy *et* le Matam
(En vous deux bons sergens atan!)
En Babiloine droit yrez:
A la mere Entrecrist direz
Qu'elle de noz ars li apreigne   435
Et ja de Dieu ne li souvaingne.
Alez y sanz nulle demeure!

ARSART DEABLE Je ne cuide jamais voir l'eure
Que cel enfant puisse veoir;
Le matin ne quier mais seoir   440
Jusque en Babiloinne venré.

LE MATAM ·IXᴱ· DEABLE Hasart, compains, je te tanré
Compaignie, se Mahons me saut.
Je ne doubte ne bas ne haut
Que bien ne saiche le passaige.   445

[Miniature No. 14]

LA DAMOISELLE Dame, regardez quel visaige [fol. 8ᵛ, col. b]
Et quieux mambres *vos*tres filz a!
Certes, des ans plus de mil a
Tieux enfés ne fu nez de mere.

91

ARSART Dame, je vien de par le pere   450
  A cest enfant que cy tenez.
  Il sera saiges *et* senez:
  De noz arts li couvient apenre.

[Miniature No. 15]

MERE ANTRECRIST A Mahon en doy graces rendre;
  Je le met en vostre baillie.   455

II. Satan Teaches Antichrist and Antichrist's Sermon:
lines 538–605 (episodes 11–12)

SATAM Je vien a toy parler, biau frere.   [fol. 10ʳ, col. a]
  J'ay grant fain de toy avancier,
  Se tu te vues a moy lancier.   540
  Je te feray le plus grant ho*m*me
  Qui onques fust, *et* saiches, co*m*me
  Je t'avray de mes gieux apris,
  Nulz homs dessuz toy n'avra pris:
  Sires seras de tout le monde.   545

[Miniature No. 18]   [fol. 10ʳ, col. b]

ANTRECRIST Par le Dieu en qui biens habonde,
  J'ay grant voulenté de l'apenre.

SATAM Or te faut bien a moy entendre:
  Il te couvient Dieu renoier
  Et a moy dou tout octroier,   550
  Et corps *et* ame tout ensamble.
  Je suis cilz par qui terre tramble.
  Je te feray estre honorez
  Seur trestouz *et* estre aourez,
  Mais que tu me couventeras   555
  Que jamés jour bien ne feras;
  Ainçois destruiras Sainte Esglise,
  Et si mettras en telle guise
  Trestoute la Cresfienté
  Que tuit seront acravanté   560
  Cil qui a toy n'obeïront
  Et qui de *Jhes*us bien diront.   [fol. 10ᵛ, col. a]
  Filz Dieu te feras appeller.
  En ne te pourra riens celer

Que tu ne puisses tout savoir. 565
Donner pourras or et avoir;
Nes les mors feras tu revivre.
Saiches, tu feras a delivre
Toute ta voulenté en terre.

ANTRECRIST Ie vueil se grant tresor *con*querre: 570
Voz homs devien de corps et d'ame.

SATAM Or te sié cy en ceste eschame
Octroier te vueil ma puissance.

[Miniature No. 19]

SATAM Je met tout en t'obeïssance
Mon povoir et le ma maigniee, 575
Qui par trestout ont seignorie. [fol. 10ᵛ, col. b]
Quanque tu devisier pourras
Fait yert si conme tu vourras:
O toy serai sanz toy laissier,
Et vers toy ferai abaissier 580
Trestouz les roys de cest païs.
En riens ne soies esbaïz:
Des or as povoir de tout faire.
Haste toy de la gent attraire,
Fay tant que ta puissance piere! 585

ANTRECRIST En terre vien de par mon pere,
Dieu tout puissant, le roy de gloire.
En moy devez vous trestuit croire,
Quar j'ay povoir sur tout le monde,
Sur ciel *et* sur la mer p*ar*fonde, 590
Quar je suis Dieux li touz puissans,
Touz biens *et* touz maux cognoissans.

[Miniature No. 20]

Or vueil que vers moy vous trayez
Et que mes oeuvres essauciez, [fol. 11ʳ, col. a]
Qu'an terre po m'avez veü, 595
Combien que vous m'aiez creü.
Je puis trestoutes choses faire,
Si suis venuz en cest repaire
Pour vous mener en paradis,
Dont li ange churent jadis. 600

93

Qui avra nulle maladie
Veigne vers moy *et* le me die,
Et je tantost le gariray
Tout yert fait quanque je diray.
Je puis trestout faire sanz doubte.

Appendix 2: List of Miniatures in Besançon 579

The following list briefly describes the subject matter of the miniatures illustrating the manuscript of the *Jour du Jugement*. Except for the first full-page miniature, all miniatures are painted within the columns of the text. Their location is identified by folio number, placement on the folio, and line number. Many images from the Besançon manuscript are available on the worldwide web at (http://www.byu.edu/~hurlbut/dscriptorium/jugement/jugement.html).

1. The Last Judgment, with General Resurrection and suffering of the damned in Hell. Fol. 2ᵛ. Full-page miniature.
2. The Preacher's sermon. Fol. 3ʳ, top left column, before l. 1.
3. The Council of Devils. Fol. 4ᵛ, right column, after l. 192.
4. Engignart and Agrappart find Antichrist's Mother. Fol. 6ʳ, top left column, before l. 283.
5. Engignart, in form of a man, approaches Antichrist's Mother in a garden. Fol. 6ʳ, bottom left column, after l. 291.
6. Engignart and Antichrist's Mother in bed. Fol. 6ᵛ, left column, after l. 321.
7. Engignart rejoins Agrappart. Fol. 6ᵛ, right column, after l. 343.
8. Engignart and Agrappart return to Hell. Fol. 7ʳ, left column, after l. 353.
9. The devils dance in Hell. Fol. 7ʳ, right column, after l. 363.
10. Antichrist's Mother and the Girl in a garden. Fol. 7ᵛ, top left column, before l. 372.
11. Antichrist's Mother in labor, assisted by the Girl. Fol. 8ʳ, left column, after l. 411.
12. The Girl holds the baby, while Antichrist's Mother lies in bed. Fol. 8ʳ, bottom left column, after l. 417.
13. Agrappart returns to Hell with news of Antichrist's birth. Fol. 8ʳ, right column, after l. 425.
14. The Girl shows the baby to Antichrist's Mother, who remains in bed. Fol. 8ᵛ, bottom left column, after l. 445.
15. Antichrist's Mother shows her baby to two devils, Hazart and Le Matam, dressed as men. Fol. 8ᵛ, right column, after l. 453.

16. Angel addresses Enoch and Elijah in the Earthly Paradise. Fol. 9^r, top right column, before l. 466.

17. Enoch and Elijah, each standing in a pulpit, preach to a large crowd. Fol. 9^v, left column, after l. 485.

18. Satan, dressed as man, approaches the young Antichrist. Fol. 10^r, top right column, before l. 546.

19. Satan gives his authority to Antichrist, who is seated. Fol. 10^v, left column, after l. 573.

20. Antichrist, dressed as a friar, preaches from a pulpit to a large crowd while others stand behind him. Fol. 10^v, right column, after l. 592.

21. Antichrist heals the kneeling Blind Man as a crowd watches. Fol. 11^r, left column, after l. 609.

22. The healed Blind Man stands and proclaims Antichrist's power. Fol. 11^r, right column, after l. 618.

23. Antichrist, seated within a Gothic building, is addressed by Annes, the Jew, while the healed Blind Man addresses crowd. Fol. 11^v, left column, after l. 629.

24. Antichrist, seated, and Annes discuss the coins engraved with Antichrist's image, while a craftsman makes the coins. Fol. 11^v, right column, after l. 653.

25. The devil, Pluto, now costumed as a man, takes a scroll from Annes, while the seated Antichrist watches. Fol. 12^r, top left column, before l. 662.

26. Pluto, as crier, reads a proclamation from the scroll, while a crowd listens. Fol. 12^r, top right column, before l. 680.

27. The Leper approaches Antichrist, seated within a Gothic building and watched by a crowd. Fol. 12^v, left column, after l. 711.

28. Antichrist cures the kneeling Leper. Fol. 12^v, bottom right column, after l. 731.

29. Antichrist, seated within a Gothic building, is approached by the Evil Bishop, while knights watch. Fol. 13^r, bottom left column, after l. 748.

30. Antichrist and crowd arrive at cemetery, where the Bishop points to a coffin. Fol. 13^v, left column, after l. 786.

31. Antichrist raises a dead body from the coffin. Fol. 13^v, right column, after l. 795.

32. The Bishop pledges support to Antichrist, seated within Gothic building, while the Resurrected Body, now clothed, enters the city gate. Fol. 14^r, left column, after l. 813.

33. Dagobert, the first king, addresses nine other kings, all crowned. Fol. 14^r, right column, after l. 831.

34. Antichrist, seated in Gothic building, is greeted by the ten kings. Fol. 15^r, left column, after l. 885.

35. The Resurrected Body, pointing to his empty coffin, tells the kings about his resurrection, while Antichrist and others watch. Fol. 15^v, left column, after l. 927.

36. The Four Poor Men approach the seated Antichrist, while the kings and others watch. Fol. 16^r, left column, after l. 955.

37. Antichrist gives clothing and other goods to the poor, while the kings watch. Fol. 16^v, left column, after l. 997.

38. King Agoulant renounces Jesus Christ and accepts Antichrist, while other kings watch. Fol. 16^v, bottom right column, after l. 1013.

39. The Jews Vivans and Marquim approach Antichrist and warn him about the preaching of Enoch and Elijah. Fol. 17^r, bottom right column, after l. 1051.

40. The Jews lead the knights to Enoch and Elijah. Fol. 17^v, left column, after l. 1063.

41. The knights, wielding swords, arrest Enoch and Elijah. Fol. 17^v, right column, after l. 1077.

42. The knights and Jews deliver Enoch and Elijah to Antichrist, who is seated in a Gothic building. Fol. 18^r, left column, after l. 1085.

43. Enoch and Elijah are attacked, while Antichrist watches. Fol. 18^v, bottom right column, after l. 1159.

44. The knights lead Enoch and Elijah away to be executed. Fol. 19^r, right column, after l. 1183.

45. Enoch and Elijah are decapitated. Fol. 19^v, left column, after l. 1195.

46. The knights return to Antichrist. Fol. 19^v, right column, after l. 1209.

47. The knights plan to capture the Pope. Fol. 20^r, left column, after l. 1229.

48. The knights seize the Pope. Fol. 20^r, right column, after l. 1243.

49. The knights take the Pope, cardinals, and other religious prisoners. Fol. 20^v, left column, after l. 1257.

50. The Pope and other religious debate with Antichrist. Fol. 21^r, left column, after l. 1295.

51. Antichrist commands Mossé to lead the Pope to prison. Fol. 22^r, top left column, before l. 1374.

52. Antichrist addresses a kneeling cardinal, while other cardinals watch. Fol. 22^r, top right column, before l. 1399.

53. The First Angel calls Enoch and Elijah from their graves, while a small group of Christians watch. Fol. 22^v, right column, after l. 1417.

54. The Second Angel leads Enoch and Elijah to the gates of Heaven, shown as a Gothic city. Fol. 22^v, bottom right column, after l. 1421.

55. Mossé attacks the Good Christian, while a crowd watches. Fol. 23^r, top right column, before l. 1442.

56. Malaquim tells Antichrist of the resurrection of Enoch and Elijah and

its effect on the crowd. Fol. 23^v, top left column, before l. 1456.

57. John the Evangelist gives out vials of wrath to four angels. Fol. 23^v, right column, after l. 1475.

58. Two angels stand before Christ enthroned in a Gothic building. Fol. 24^r, left column, after l. 1503.

59. The First Angel, emerging from a cloud, pours a vial of wrath over those who worshipped Antichrist. Fol. 24^r, right column, after l. 1517.

60. The First Angel continues to pour a vial over many dead bodies. Fol. 24^v, top left column, before l. 1522.

61. The Second Angel pours a vial of wrath over knights. Fol. 24^v, left column, after l. 1527.

62. The Second Angel continues to pour a vial over a large group of dead knights. Fol. 24^v, right column, after l. 1533.

63. Three angels kneel before Christ in a Gothic building. Fol. 25^r, left column, after l. 1555.

64. The Fourth Angel pours its vial over Antichrist, who lies on top of his dead followers. Fol. 25^r, right column, after l. 1569.

65. The Fifth Angel pours a vial of wrath over the throne of the beast and the Jews. Fol. 25^v, left column, after l. 1586.

66. Beelzebub leaves the body that had been falsely resurrected. Fol. 25^v, right column, after l. 1601.

67. The Sixth Angel pours a vial of wrath over the powerful and uncharitable. Fol. 26^r, left column, after l. 1615.

68. The Blind Man, having lost his sight again, prays to Christ, looking down from a cloud, for forgiveness. Fol. 26^r, right column, after l. 1633.

69. Four devils take council. Fol. 26^v, top left column, before l. 1644.

70. The devils arm themselves for war. Fol. 26^v, top right column, before l. 1660.

71. The ten kings kneel before the Virgin Mary, while Christ is enthroned in a Gothic arch. Fol. 27^r, top right column, before l. 1692.

72. The Cherubim and Seraphim kneel before the Virgin Mary and plead for her intercession. Fol. 27^v, left column, after l. 1725.

73. John the Baptist and two angels kneel before the Virgin Mary. Fol. 27^v, bottom right column, after l. 1743.

74. Paul and other saints kneel before the Virgin Mary. Fol. 28^r, right column, after l. 1771.

75. John and the other Evangelists kneel before Christ enthroned in a Gothic building. Fol. 29^r, bottom right column, after l. 1873.

76. Christ sends the Four Evangelists, who hold trumpets, into the four corners of the world. Fol. 29^v, top right column, before l. 1896.

77. The Four Evangelists blow their trumpets over several coffins. Fol. 29^v, bottom right column, after l. 1905.

78. The Evil Bishop and Abbess rise from their coffins. Fol. 30^v, top left column, before l. 1954.

79. King Agoulant and other dead bodies rise from coffins. Fol. 30^v, top right column, before l. 1970.

80. The Usurer and his household rise from their coffins, while Christ watches and judges them. Fol. 31^v, left column, after l. 2029.

81. Christ sends the Usurers to Hell with the devil Hazart. Fol. 32^r, left column, after l. 2075.

82. The Evil Bishop and Prioress speak from their coffins, while a devil watches. Fol. 32^v, bottom left column, after l. 2129.

83. Christ in judgment shows his wounds, two angels above hold the cross and lance, while the resurrected kneel below. Fol. 33^v, top left column, before l. 2203.

84. Christ, enthroned and showing his wounds, watches Peter and Paul judge the evil on Christ's left. Fol. 34^r, left column, after l. 2234.

85. Christ, enthroned and showing his wounds, watches Andrew and James judge the righteous on Christ's right. Fol. 34^r, top right column, before l. 2247.

86. Christ, enthroned and showing his wounds, watches Simon judge the evil, while the righteous stand on Christ's right. Fol. 35^r, left column, after l. 2310.

87. Christ addresses the righteous on his right, while the evil wait on his left. Fol. 35^r, bottom right column, after l. 2340.

88. The devil Rapillart leads a large group of damned to the gates of Hell, where they are met by Belial. Fol. 35^r, left column, after l. 2389.

89. John, Luke, and Paul address the saved. Fol. 36^v, left column, after l. 2421.

Appendix 3: The Music in Besançon 579

by Keith Glaeske

The *Jour du Jugement*, found in Besançon, Bibliothèque Municipale, MS 579, contains three examples of music, each of which is meant to be performed by an angel. The music appears in late medieval notation for plainchant: black square notation arranged upon a red four-line staff with C-clefs. Although Émile Roy acknowledged in his edition of the play that these melodies were adapted from medieval Latin hymns, he did not comment upon the unusual combination of vernacular texts and Latin hymn melodies.

According to Roy, the hymn melodies preserved on folios 8^v–9^r, 22^v, and 33^v of Besançon 529 are *Aeterne Rex altissime* ("Eternal King, most high God"), *Veni Creator Spiritus* ("Come, Creator Spirit"), and *Urbs Jerusalem beata* ("Blessed Jerusalem city").[1] The first hymn probably dates from the tenth century; its composer is unknown. It was intended to be sung during Matins on Ascension Day. The second hymn also can be found in manuscripts from the tenth century, but the composition probably dates from as early as the ninth century. Although its authorship is still unknown, it has been variously ascribed to Ambrose, Gregory the Great, Charlemagne, and Rabanus Maurus. Liturgically, it is assigned to Vespers on Pentecost; due to the influence of Cluny, it was also sung at Terce on that feast (cf. Acts 2:15).[2] From the eleventh century onwards, *Veni Creator Spiritus* was also sung at the ordination of priests, the consecration of bishops, and the dedication of churches. The third hymn was likewise sung at the dedication of a church during the hour of Vespers. It dates from the eighth or ninth century, and its composer is also unknown.

Although hymns have long been an integral part of Christian worship, especially as elements of the Divine Office, they seldom are recorded in medieval antiphoners and breviaries, which typically give only textual incipits of the hymns, often without music. Nevertheless, the three hymns which serve as the basis for the songs in the *Jour du Jugement* appear in full in Cambrai, Médiathèque Municipale, Impr. XVI C 4, an antiphoner record-

---

[1] *Jour du Jugement*, ed. Roy, 14–15. The three hymns are catalogued in Hesbert, ed., *Corpus antiphonalium officii*, vol. 4, as nos. 8255, 8407, and 8405, respectively. The entire texts for *Aeterne Rex altissime* and *Veni Creator Spiritus*, with English translations, can be found in Connelly, *Hymns of the Roman Liturgy*, 102–5 and 106–7, respectively; the text for *Urbs Jerusalem beata* appears in Blume, ed., *Analecta hymnica medii aevi*, vol. 51, 110–12.

[2] Connelly, *Hymns*, 107.

ing the Divine Office at Cambrai Cathedral printed in Paris by Simon Vostre, ca. 1508–1518.[3] The music on fols. 8^v–9^r of Besançon 579 (*"Enoc, Enoc, et vous, Elie,"* ll. 456ff.) follows the contour of *Aeterne Rex altissime* in Cambrai XVI, although the original hymn melody has been simplified in the play in order to fit the vernacular text.[4] The melody used on fol. 22^v of Besançon 579 (*"Vous qui avez la mort soufferte,"* ll. 1410ff.), however, follows the melody of *Veni Creator Spiritus* in Cambrai XVI almost note for note.[5] A comparison of the melody preserved on fol. 33^v of Besançon 579 (*"Venez tuit oïr la santance,"* ll. 2203ff.) with that of the *Urbs Jerusalem beata* of Cambrai XVI, fol. 88^v, however, shows almost no correspondance between the two. The music in Besançon 579 begins a fourth lower than the hymn in Cambrai XVI, ends on *e* instead of *f*, and encompasses a different range (*c* to *c′* instead of *B* to *b*). Although this contradicts Roy's assertion that although the third chant in the play "est quelque peu altérée," it still is "très reconnaissable" (p. 15), it should be noted that even in the liturgical tradition the melody for *Urbs Jerusalem beata* is far from stable. A different melody for the same hymn is preserved in Paris, Bibliothèque National de France, MS lat. 15182, the second of a two-volume breviary from Notre Dame Cathedral in Paris.[6] Finding a melody of *Urbs Jerusalem beata*—or the melody of another hymn— that better matches the music used for *Venez tuit oïr la santance* in the play might provide some insight into the original provenance of the *Jour du Jugement.*

The use of Latin liturgical music with Latin texts is well attested in medieval vernacular drama. The *Jour du Jugement* itself alludes to this practice when St. Paul declares at the end of the play "Let us now sing *Te*

---

[3] Both text and music for *Aeterne Rex altissime, Veni Creator Spiritus,* and *Urbs Jerusalem beata* appear on fols. 59^v, 67^v, and 88^v, respectively of Cambrai XVI; the melody for *Aeterne Rex altissime* appears twice, also being used for *Verbum supernum* (fol. 74^v; cf. *Jour du Jugement,* ed. Roy, 15). For information about Cambrai XVI see the introduction to Barbara Haggh, et al., *Two Cambrai Antiphoners: Cambrai, Médiathèque Municipale, 38 and Impr. XVI C 4,* Musicological Studies LV/4 (Ottawa: Institute of Mediaeval Music, 1995), xxi–xxx.

[4] For example, the opening phrase of *g g -a-b-c′-b-a g-f* in *Aeterne Rex altissime* is reduced to *g g -a-c′ a-g-f* in *Enoc, Enoc, et vous, Elie.*

[5] The only exception occurs at the beginning of the second line of *Vous qui avez la mort soufferte* (repeated in the sixth line), which modifies the original *c′ a-g g -a c′* to *c′ c′-b g-a-c′.*

[6] The melody of *Urbs beata Jerusalem* in Paris, BNF, lat. 15182 has a range of *e* to *e′* and a final of *a;* see fol. 162^v. Indexes of Cambrai XVI and Paris, BNF, lat. 15182 can be accessed from the CANTUS database on the World Wide Web at ⟨http://www.cua.edu/ musu/cantus⟩; a hard copy of the CANTUS index of Cambrai XVI has been published (see n. 3 above), and the index of Paris, BNF, lat. 15182, by Susan Kidwell, with an introduction by Rebecca Baltzer, is forthcoming from the Institute of Mediaeval Music.

Deum'' (l. 2437). Similarily, the use of non-liturgical music with vernacular texts also occurs in medieval French drama (e.g., Adam de la Halle's *Le Jeu de Robin et de Marion*). However, Besançon 579 is a rare example of the combination of traditional music from a Latin liturgical setting with newly composed vernacular texts. Moreover, the French text is not simply a translation of the original Latin text; it is a part of the dialogue of the play itself which has been set to pre-existing liturgical music. As a result, the music in the *Jour du Jugement* fulfills a different purpose than the music in most medieval vernacular drama: it does not provide an interlude or bring the play to a close, but rather serves to expand and embellish the dialogue. The merging of liturgical music and vernacular text can perhaps best be explained by the performer chosen for all three instances—an angel. Although angels praise God in song, they also act as his messengers to humankind. Therefore liturgical music may have been deemed more appropriate than the use of secular music to emphasize the special nature of the angelic speeches.

ENOC, ENOC, ET VOUS, ELIE

E - NOC, E - NOC, ET VOUS, E - LI - E,

DE PAR DIEU YS - SEZ DE SE - ANZ!

A - LEZ PRE - SCHIER AUX MES - CREANS

LA LOY DIEU ES - TA - BLIE EN TER - RE.

IS - SEZ HORS ET A - LEZ EN GUER - RE

QUAR, POUR BIEN DI - RE, MORT SE - REZ,

MAIS A - PRES RE - SU - SCI - TE - REZ.

CER - TAINS SUIS QUE BI - EN LE SA - VEZ.

VOUS QUI AVEZ LA MORT SOUFFERTE

VOUS QUI A - VEZ LA MORT SOUF - ER - TE

POUR JHE -SU -CRIST, LE FIL MA - RIE,

DE PAR LI RE - VE - NEZ EN VI -E.

POUR LI A -VEZ ES - TÉ MAR - TIR,

O -REN -DROIT VOUS FAUST DE - PAR - TIR

DE CE VIL ET COR -ROM-PU MON-DE

OU -QUEL IL N'A NUL -LE RIENS MON-DE,

ET SA EN PA - RA - DIS MON -TER.

VENEZ TUIT OIT LA SANTANCE

VE -NEZ TUIT O - IR LA SAN-TAN-CE

DOU SEI - GNEUR, DOU DOUZ ROY BE - NI - GNE

VEEZ VOUS CI EN PRE - SENT LE SI - NE

OU SOUF - FRI MORT ET PAS - SI - ON

POUR LA VOS - TRE RE - DAMP - TI - ON

A VOUS QUI DES - SER - VI L'A - VEZ?

Bibliography

Primary Texts

Adso of Montier-en-Der. *Libellus de Antichristo.* Trans. Bernard McGinn. *Apocalyptic Spirituality.* New York: Paulist Press, 1979. Pp. 81–96.

Augustine. *City of God.* Trans. Henry Bettenson, ed. David Knowles. Baltimore: Penguin, 1972.

Berliner Weltgerichtsspiel: Augsburger Buch vom Jüngsten Gericht. Ed. Ursula Schulze. Littera: Göppinger Beiträge zur Textgeschichte, 114. Göppingen: Kümmerle, 1991.

Bevington, David, ed. *Medieval Drama.* Boston: Houghton Mifflin, 1975.

Blume, Clemens, ed. *Analecta hymnica medii aevi.* Leipzig: Reisland, 1908.

Boveland, Karin, et al. *Der Antichrist und Die Fünfzehn Zeichen vor dem Jüngsten Gericht.* Hamburg: Friedrich Wittig, 1979.

The Chester Mystery Cycle. Ed. R. M. Luminansky and David Mills. EETS ss 3. London: Oxford Univ. Press, 1974.

Churer Weltgerichtsspiele: Nach der Handschrift des Staatsarchivs Graubünden Chur Ms. B 1521. Ed. Ursula Schulze. Berlin: Erich Schmidt, 1993.

Connelly, Joseph. *Hymns of the Roman Liturgy.* Westminster, Md.: Newman Press, 1957.

Elliott, John R., Jr., and Graham A. Runnalls, eds. *The Baptism and Temptation of Christ: The First Day of a Medieval French Passion Play.* New Haven: Yale Univ. Press, 1978.

Des Entkrist Vasnacht. Ed. Friederike Christ-Kutter. *Frühe Schweizerspiele.* Altdeutsche Übungstexte 19. Bern: Francke, 1963.

Gardiner, Eileen, ed. *Visions of Heaven and Hell before Dante.* New York: Italica, 1989.

Jacobus de Voragine. *Legenda aurea.* Trans. William Granger Ryan, as *The Golden Legend: Readings on the Saints.* 2 vols. Princeton: Princeton Univ. Press, 1993.

Jerome. *Commentary on Daniel.* Trans. Gleason L. Archer, Jr. Grand Rapids: Baker Book House, 1958.

Le Jour du Jugement: Mystère français sur le Grand Schisme. Ed. Émile Roy. Études sur le théâtre français au xive siècle. Paris: Emile Bouillon, 1902.

Le Jugement Dernier (Lo Jutgamen General): Drame provençal du XVe siècle. Ed. Moshé Lazar. Paris: Klincksieck, 1971.

Künzelsauer Fronleichnamspiel. Ed. Peter K. Liebenow. Berlin: Walter de Gruyter, 1969.

Ludus de Antichristo. Trans. John Wright under the title *The Play of Antichrist.* Toronto: Pontifical Institute of Mediaeval Studies, 1967.

Meredith, Peter, and John E. Tailby, eds. *The Staging of Religious Drama in Europe in the Later Middle Ages: Texts and Documents in English Translation.* Early Drama, Art, and Music Monograph Series, 4. Kalamazoo: Medieval Institute Publications, 1983.

Le mystère de l'Antéchrist et du Jugement de Dieu. Ed. Louis Gros, *Étude sur le Mystère del'Antéchrist et du Jugement de Dieu joué à Modane en 1580 et en 1606.* Chambéry: Réunies, 1962.

Le mystère de la passion nostre Seigneur: du manuscrit 1131 de la Bibliothèque Sainte-Geneviève. Textes litteraires français, 206. Ed. Graham A. Runnalls. Geneva: Droz, 1974.

La Passion du Palatinus: Mystère du xive siècle. Ed. Grace Frank. CFMA. Paris: Champion, 1922. Reproduced with intro. and trans. into Modern French by Jacques Ribard. Paris: Champion, 1992.

Perugia Last Judgment Play. Ed. Vincenzo de Bartholomaeis. *Laude drammatiche e rappresentazione sacre.* Florence: Felice le Monnier, 1943. 1:35–52.

Robert de Boron. *Merlin.* Ed. Alexandre Micha. Geneva: Droz, 1979.

Rutebeuf. *Le Miracle de Théophile.* In *Medieval French Plays,* translated by Richard Axton and John Stevens, 165–92. Oxford: Basil Blackwell, 1971.

Secondary Sources

Aichele, Klaus. *Das Antichristdrama des Mittelalters der Reformation und Gegenreformation.* The Hague: Martinus Nijhoff, 1974.

Andrus, Toni W. "The Devil on the Medieval Stage in France." Ph.D. diss. Syracuse Univ., 1979.

Bevington, David, et al., eds. *"Homo, Memento Finis": The Iconography of Just Judgment in Medieval Art and Drama.* Early Drama, Art, and Music Monograph Series, 6. Kalamazoo: Medieval Institute Publications, 1985.

Blumenfeld-Kosinksi, Renate. "Illustration as Commentary in Late Medieval Images of Antichrist's Birth," *Deutsche Vierteljahrsschrift für Literaturwissenschaft und Geistesgeschichte* 63 (1989): 589–607.

Castan, Auguste, ed. *Catalogue général des manuscrits des bibliothèques publiques des France-Départements 32, Besançon.* Vol. 1. Paris: Plon, 1897.

Chocheyras, Jacques. *Le Théâtre religieux en Savoie au 16e siècle.* Publications romanes et françaises, 115. Geneva: Droz, 1971.

Cohen, Gustave. *Histoire de la mise en scène dans le théâtre religieux français du Moyen Âge.* Paris: Honoré Champion, 1951.

————. "Le Jour du Jugement dans le théâtre français au Moyen-Âge." *Convivium* 25 (1957): 268–75.

Cornagliotti, Anna. "I diavoli nel teatro italiano dalle origini al XVI secolo." *Diavoli e mostri in scena dal Medio Evo al Rinascimento*. Rome: Centro studi sul teatro mediovale e rinascimentale, 1988. Pp. 97–168.

Davidson, Clifford, and Thomas H. Seiler, eds. *The Iconography of Hell.* Early Drama, Art, and Music Monograph Series, 17. Kalamazoo: Medieval Institute Publications, 1992.

DuBruck, Edelgard. "The Devil and Hell in Medieval French Drama: Prolegomena." *Romania* 100 (1979): 165–79.

Emmerson, Richard Kenneth. *Antichrist in the Middle Ages: A Study of Medieval Apocalypticism, Art, and Literature.* Seattle: Univ. of Washington Press, 1981.

————. "'Nowe Ys Common This Daye': Enoch and Elias, Antichrist, and the Structure of the Chester Cycle." In Bevington, et al., eds., *"Homo, Memento Finis."* Pp. 89–120.

————. "Wynkyn de Worde's *Byrthe and Lyfe of Antechryst* and Popular Eschatology on the Eve of the English Reformation," *Mediaevalia* 14 (1988): 281–311.

Emmerson, Richard Kenneth, and Ronald B. Herzman. *The Apocalyptic Imagination in Medieval Literature.* Philadelphia: Univ. of Pennsylvania Press, 1992.

Foxton, Cynthia. "Hell and the Devil in the Medieval French Drama: Vision of Damnation or Hope for Salvation?" In *Dies Illa: Death in the Middle Ages,* edited by Jane H. M. Taylor. Liverpool: Francis Cairns, 1984. Pp. 71–79.

Frank, Grace. *The Medieval French Drama.* Oxford: Clarendon Press, 1954.

Haslinghuis, Edward J. *De Duivel in het Drama.* Leiden: Gebroeders van der Hoek, 1912.

Hesbert, René-Jean. *Corpus antiphonalium officii.* Rerum ecclesiasticarum documenta, Series maior, Fontes 10. Rome: Herder, 1970.

Hughes, Robert. *Heaven and Hell in Western Art.* New York: Stein and Day, 1968.

Iancu-Agou, Daniel. "Le diable et le Juif: Représentation médiévales iconographiques et écrites." In *Le diable au Moyen Âge: doctrine, problèmes moraux, représentations.* Senefiance 6, Publications du C.U.E.R.M.A. Paris: Honoré Champion, 1979. Pp. 259–76.

Knight, Alan E. *Aspects of Genre in Late Medieval French Drama.* Manchester: Manchester Univ. Press, 1983.

Konigson, Elie. *L'espace théâtral médiéval.* Paris: CNRS, 1975.

Langmuir, Gavin. I. *Toward a Definition of Antisemitism.* Berkeley: Univ. of California Press, 1990.

Leigh, David J. "The Doomsday Mystery Play: An Eschatological Morality." *Modern Philology* 67 (1969–70): 211–33.

Lieblein, Leanore. "Flexible Iconography: The Experience of the Spectator of Medieval Religious Drama." In *La langue, le texte, le jeu: Perspectives sur le Théâtre médiéval*. Le moyen français 19. Montreal: Ceres, 1986. Pp. 135–47.

Lifschitz-Golden, Manya. *Les Juifs dans la littérature française du Moyen Âge (mystères, miracles, chroniques)*. New York: Institute of French Studies, Columbia Univ., 1935.

McGinn, Bernard. *Antichrist: Two Thousand Years of the Human Fascination with Evil*. San Francisco: HarperCollins, 1994.

———. "Portraying Antichrist in the Middle Ages." In *The Use and Abuse of Eschatology in the Middle Ages*. Ed. Werner Verbeke, Daniel Verhelst, Andries Welkenhuysen. Leuven: Leuven Univ. Press, 1988. Pp. 1–48.

Moisan, André. *Répertoire des noms propres de personnes et de lieux cités dans les chançons de geste françaises et les oeuvres étrangères dérivées*. Publications romanes et françaises 173. 2 tomes in 5 vols. Geneva: Droz, 1986.

Owen, D. D. R. *The Vision of Hell: Infernal Journeys in Medieval French Literature*. Edinburgh: Scottish Academic Press, 1970.

Palmer, Barbara D. "The Inhabitants of Hell: Devils." In Davidson and Seiler, eds., *Iconography of Hell*. Pp. 20–40.

Petit de Julleville, Louis. *Histoire du théâtre en France: Les Mystères*. 2 vols. 1880; repr. Geneva: Slatkine, 1968.

Rastall, Richard. "The Sounds of Hell." In Davidson and Seiler, eds., *Iconography of Hell*. Pp. 102–31.

Rey-Flaud, Henri. *Le Cercle magique*. Paris: Gallimard, 1973.

Roy, Émile. *Le Mystère de la passion en France du xive au xvie siècle*. 1903; repr. Geneva: Slatkine, 1974.

Runnalls, Graham A. "Form and Meaning in Medieval Religious Drama." In *Littera et Sensus: Essays on Form and Meaning in Medieval French Literature Presented to John Fox*. Ed. D. A. Trotter. Exeter: Univ. of Exeter Publications, 1989. Pp. 95–107.

———. "Towards a Typology of Medieval French Play Manuscripts." In *The Editor and the Text*. Ed. Philip E. Bennett and Graham A. Runnalls. Edinburgh: Edinburgh Univ. Press, 1990. Pp. 96–113.

Russell, Jeffrey Burton. *Lucifer: The Devil in the Middle Ages*. Ithaca, NY: Cornell Univ. Press, 1984.

Sheingorn, Pamela. "'For God Is Such a Doomsman': Origins and Development of the Theme of Last Judgment." In Bevington, et al., eds., *"Homo, Memento Finis."* Pp. 15–58.

———. "'Who Can Open the Doors of His Face?' The Iconography of Hell Mouth." In Davidson and Seiler, eds., *The Iconography of Hell*. Pp. 1–19.

Sheingorn, Pamela, and David Bevington. "'Alle This Was Token Domysday to Drede': Visual Signs of Last Judgment in the Corpus Christi Cycles and in Late Gothic Art." In Bevington, et al., eds., "*Homo, Memento Finis.*" Pp. 121–45.

Stevens, Martin. *Four Middle English Mystery Cycles: Textual, Contextual and Critical Interpretations*. Princeton: Princeton Univ. Press, 1987.

Trachtenberg, Joshua. *The Devil and the Jews: The Medieval Conception of the Jew and its Relation to Modern Antisemitism*. New Haven: Yale Univ. Press, 1943.

Tydeman, William. *The Theatre in the Middle Ages*. Cambridge: Cambridge Univ. Press, 1978.

Valois, Noël. Review of Roy's *Le Jour du Jugement*. *Journal des Savants*, n.s. 1 (1903): 677–86.

Wright, Rosemary Muir. *Art and Antichrist in Medieval Europe*. Manchester: Manchester Univ. Press, 1995.